André Lannes

Scientific and philosophical essay

Deciphering

our world

from what we know

today

Translated from French by Lucy Teasdale

2020

Table of contents

▟ Preface

I can claim no credentials for prefacing this impressive scholarly work other than my friendship for André Lannes.

We met as fellow lecturers on the occasion of two interdisciplinary seminars chaired by Henri Callat in Carcassonne: in 2015 for 'Le temps des fraternités' (the age of fraternities) and in 2016 for 'De la violence du monde' (on the violence of the world). This Sisyphus of commitment and cynicism brought together humanists, whether curious or militant, to re-examine these problems in the light of today's knowledge. André Lannes brought the physicist's viewpoint to these issues, measuring history on the time scale and dimensions of the Universe, and positioning today's man in the adventure of the hominids while linking him to the underlying reality of the quantum whirlwind that constitutes the world and life.

After graduating in physical sciences he completed a PhD in electron microscopy before being appointed Head of Research at the CNRS, the French National Centre for Scientific Research, in the Department of Sciences of the Universe. He then spent four years as the Deputy Director of the Toulouse Astrophysics Laboratory at the Midi-Pyrénées Observatory.

His research on the image-object relationship and the limitations of its inversion led him to take a year-long sabbatical at the University of California, Berkeley where he explored all aspects of image reconstruction, notably in the fields of astronomy and geophysics. This research questioned the truth of our perceptions.

His thoughts and ideas on human problems are based, as far as possible, on the great advances of twentieth-century scientific thought and on his interdisciplinary research thus questioning the certainties, representations and values that everyone holds within themselves to varying degrees.

His approach reminds me of those Greek 'physicists' and 'physiologists' who, from as early as the sixth century B.C.E. sought the causes of natural phenomena, such as ANAXIMANDER who used the terms *apeiron* (the indefinite) and *archē* (the principle of all things). For André Lannes, quantum physics is this *archē*. Like the philosophy of 'physiologists', which turned its back on myths and the supernatural, and EPICURUS in the fourth century B.C.E. who linked physics to ethics, André Lannes in the manner of LUCRETIUS (a great admirer of EPICURUS) explores the complex questions of knowledge, individual and collective behaviour, social organisation, and possible human welfare in the light of quantum physics.

This approach guided the writing of this popular scientific and philosophical essay entitled: Deciphering our World Today. It can be seen as a modern *De rerum natura* based on an inversion of Plato's allegory of the cave: the darkness lurking within the depths of Nature is its reality while the light on its surface is its appearance.

The reader will find a presentation (prepared with a pedagogical concerns) of the fundamental notions stemming from the scientific revolution, and the repercussions on our ideas and representations. The instability and sheer whimsy of the quantum world prompts us to look differently at evil, violence, the disorders of Nature and humans, inequalities, the paranormal and the unexpected. In other words, do we humans have agency or are our notions of free will, freedom, responsibility, equality, progress and so forth just empty words? This certainly casts additional doubt on the formation of judgement and thought, as well as arousing pessimism about our mastery of civilisation: *a return to tragedy through science!*

André Lannes, an avid reader of SPINOZA, expresses a radical mistrust of all doctrines, whether political, economic or theological, and especially for the religions he knew, as a teenager, the Dionysism of the charismatics in an exacerbated mystical environment.

Fortunately, the author discerns a glimmer of hope, albeit minor and partial, in this gloomy picture. Quantum potential can also generate harmonious achievements in everything related to art, spirituality and the virtues. Evolution (from the hominids to today's man), in which epigenetics records these achievements, is already giving rise to this hope. And the humble researcher, who is aware that we probably only know less than five per cent of all things in Nature and life, and who leaves a great deal of room for doubt, finally expresses, as a man, an expectation. As both a musician sensitive to emotional interactions and a scientist awed by the beauty of mathematics and theoretical physics, the author believes in a systemic reaction against the devouring forces of our technical modernity to gradually record new harmonies in our genetic heritage.

The complex concept of the 'incomplete' and the beautiful Giralducian image of the dawn echo an allegory of HESIOD inspired by HOMER i.e. that of the jar which still contains the *elpis* or the expectation of hope after all the evils of the world have escaped.

Lucien Bordaux,
Honorary Lecturer at the
Université Toulouse – Jean JAURÈS

Acknowledgements

Many discussions contributed to the writing of this popular scientific and philosophical essay.

Firstly, I would like to thank Lucien Bordaux who kindly read all the drafts and wrote the preface. In particular, I would like to thank him for his extremely astute remarks on the Pre-Socratics, the Hellenistic period and certain New Testament texts.

My colleague, José-Philippe Pérez, kindly shared his comments on aspects of popular science involving general relativity and quantum physics. I would like to thank him warmly thinking, in particular, about our complementary scientific journeys from gaining our teaching qualifications in physical sciences to our respective theses on electron microscopy.

We enjoyed many discussions with Franc Bardou on the concepts of Being, the soul and the mind as described in this essay. May he also be warmly thanked.

Henri Callat recently departed this world. Despite our very varied backgrounds, he was able to bring us together, encouraging us to discuss and probe everything we could think of about the world and life. So, these lines were written with him in mind.

◤ Foreword

Questioning concepts related to the things of this world is an unwelcome privilege of the human condition, yet it is a privilege as to do so you must be free from hunger, thirst and toothache. Moreover, you must have a brain in good working order, with a light on almost every floor, which is far from being clearly established. Yet for those of us lucky enough to possess such a brain, this privilege is a burden because thinking about these concepts means questioning their validity and their possible sense, which is not always easy. In fact, we may ask ourselves whether we should even try. Perhaps it would be better just to feel things as humans and act accordingly. Yet it is precisely because of this that a yawning chasm gapes. What exactly does it mean 'to feel things as humans'? In an attempt to answer this question, we must examine 'the nature of things'. Here, we are explicitly referring to the poem written by LUCRETIUS in the first century B.C.E. entitled: *De rerum natura*.

Therefore, questioning the things in our world ultimately requires us to decipher our world one way or another, implicitly or even better explicitly. And to decipher our world 'today', we must consider the myriad facets of human culture over the past four millennia including the scientific advances of the twentieth century and especially those that have changed how we view time and things from the extremely small to the extremely large. In this context, the word 'today' reminds us that in the early twenty-first century we are still nowhere near the end of the history of science. For example, what about the validity of string theory or loop quantum gravity? What should we think about what we call the 'Big Bang'? While it was certainly a phenomenal transition, could it not have been a rebound from another Universe into our own, or was it something even more tenuous? Nobody can say for sure.

Can we ignore all these considerations and, in particular, their impact on everything related to life? We can but we must not then be surprised if the majority of our so-called values i.e. those on which our lives and societies are founded (notably via religious, economic and political institutions) very often turn out to be in flagrant contradiction to the reality of who we really are or what we will become.

In a world that is ceaselessly moving and vibrating, and which can not simply be reduced to what we perceive of it, we must strive to decipher it and experience it through more sophisticated representations. Therefore, we will talk about our human gaze on Nature, the dynamics of our Universe, matter, fundamental interactions, the Sun, the Earth, life and sense as it emerges within us.

Firstly, it is important to attempt to clarify what we mean by Nature i.e. that which resulted from 'our Big Bang'. Enigmatically, in the absence of a more precise definition, we could say it is 'the vibrant dynamic substance that underlies the form and metamorphosis of all things'; the substance or noumenon [1] of the phenomena we perceive from it. Is this the Totality of Being? Nothing could be less certain. Nature may be a remarkable achievement of Being but that does not mean it has reached its full potential. In this scientific and philosophical essay, the term 'achievement' does not mean creation, rather it indicates a process of random (uncertain) transition. Moreover, the term 'Being' does not refer to a conscious entity but simply to the fact that there seems to be something rather than nothing (as opposed to non-Being). All the more reason to meticulously analyse everything we can perceive from Nature as this might, if we are lucky, allow us to glimpse this elusive Being.

Deciphering the world in this very open framework (knowing what we know and what we do not know today) is incredibly difficult. Moreover, there can be no philosophy worthy of its name, and therefore open to criticism, without an in-depth analysis via the biological systems of our brains of the relationship between the real and heavily filtered images we have of the world. In this respect, it should be remembered that the brain is a complex biological system which, when in good working order, has several embedded, albeit limited, analysis subsystems including our five senses (to name but these), as well as memory, consciousness and thought. These systems provide us with abstract recon-structed images of the objects-subjects of our representations of the world.

---

1. Here, we are referring to KANT's concept of noumenon i.e. everything that sensi-tivity to phenomena can not achieve even via our most sophisticated experimental approaches.

With regard to thought in particular, we are entitled to question its limitations in terms of perception and resolution as naturally this varies from one individual to another and, more generally, from one culture or civilisation to another. In fact, here we come to the very heart of the problem as it is addressed in this scientific and philosophical essay.

In this context, it is also worth noting the limitations of neuroscience, which is only just beginning to take shape with Transcranial Magnetic Stimulation (TMS) and Functional Magnetic Resonance Imaging (fMRI) in particular. In the living tree of our biosphere, evolutionary mechanisms have shaped how our brains work over millions of years. These sciences are a long way off from understanding the teeming multitudes, animals, humans or even an individual.

The titles of the ten points examined in this popular scientific and philosophical essay are as follows:
1) The emergence of thought among hominids
2) The yawning chasm of the thing-in-itself
3) Fundamental representations
4) In the cosmic forges of gravitation
5) The constructive processes of quantum biology
6) The evolution of representations
7) On the violence of life
8) Nature's harmonies
9) Beliefs and spirituality
10) Acting in a fraternity of the incomplete

In Point 1, we sketch a succinct picture of the spacetime stage in which hominids first began to think. In this context, we will analyse the process of how an idea is formed.

The relationship between Nature, as an object, and the images (in the broadest meaning) which humankind can perceive from it, can not be inverted [2]; we will examine this fundamental scientific and philosophical question in Point 2.

In the first popular science point (Point 3), we will then introduce the four fundamental interactions of Nature. The second point focuses on the processes involved in the emergence of life in the cosmic forges of gravitation (Point 4).

We will then indicate in Point 5 how today's physicists and biologists attempt to understand the rich texture of living organisms, as well as their fabulous and dynamic achievements. Changes in our vision of the things in this world show that the representations (inevitably incomplete) of the same object-subject are nevertheless hierarchical; we will thus see in Point 6 that not everything is equal.

In the previously defined physical framework, we will then examine (in Points 7 and 8) how the violence of life co-exists with the harmonies found in Nature. In Point 9 we will examine the question of the existence of god; this poorly posed question all too often masks the compelling need for a spirituality which is accessible to all and which would allow us to perceive the veiled harmonies of Being.

---

2. The relationship 'A gives B' is invertible if there is a relationship in which 'B gives A'.

The concept of a fraternity of the incomplete, as presented in Point 10, is dictated to us by the observation of Nature's awe inspiring achievements, which unfortunately occur all too rarely.

The reader may wonder why the popular science points (3 and 4) are treated as such in the essay i.e. sometimes densely and abstractly, and at other times vividly and in detail. The reason is simple: in Point 3 it is necessary to define a solid and well-structured scientific framework but, above all, to show in Point 4 that life is simply one of Nature's achievements like any other; it is not a miracle.

So, instead of navel-gazing, perhaps we humans should turn our attention to all Nature's myriad achievements. These prodigious phenomena can seem a long way from our existential concerns but if we gave them more thought, as well as considering the insignificance [3] of our own condition in terms of the tree of life, our perception of our presence in this world would be very different. In particular, education would have a stronger impact on the minds of adolescents, the problems of global overpopulation, hunger and lack of clean drinking water would be resolved naturally and, in the medium term, our biosphere would regain its fundamental dynamic balances. In any case, this is what the author believes.

---

3. https //www.youtube.com/watch ?v=stCxLxBMjYA, watch the full ARTE documentary entitled "Une espèce à part" (A species apart).

◤ Point 1

The emergence of thought among hominids

It is impossible to think about the world without first questioning the presence of humans in it. Therefore, let us begin by sketching a succinct picture of the spacetime stage on which hominids first emerged and gradually began to think.

1. The spacetime stage

For – let us say – 50 years, humankind has realised that one to two million years ago it gradually crawled onto the stage of an incredible spectacle that started with a phenomenal 'clap of thunder' around 13.8 billion years ago: the 'Big Bang'.

To give us a more concrete idea of the scale of this fabulous spectacle and to plot some of its major episodes in time, let us position today at point 'A' on an axis oriented towards the future.

From this point, let us travel along this axis towards the past [1] at the speed of one millimetre a year. After travelling

---

1. It is in this direction that research is carried out in the fields of geology and palaeontology in particular.

13.8 billion years and therefore [2] 13,800 km, we finally arrive, after this incredibly long voyage, at point 'B' and the Big Bang, which is a long way in anyone's book [3]!

In this return to the origins, the positions of the events below are given in relation to point A:

a) The major scientific breakthroughs of the twentieth century between 5 and 12 cm.

b) The Age of Enlightenment at 40 cm.

c) Jesus of Nazareth at 2 m.

d) The pre-Socratic philosophers between 2.4 and 2.7 m.

e) The first signs of thought in homo sapiens between 40 and 100 m.

f) Their slow arrival onto the world stage between 1 and 2 km.

g) The addition of two twigs on the primate branch of our tree of life i.e. hominids on one, and chimpanzees (and their cousins) on the second at around 8 km.

h) The disappearance of the dinosaurs at approximately 66 km.

i) The appearance of the first primates between 70 and 80 km.

j) The Jurassic period between 135 and 203 km.

k) The appearance of the first dinosaurs at around 240 km.

l) The first vertebrate land animals at about 380 km.

m) The first signs of life in the warm seas at 3,800 km.

---

2. Indeed, 1 km = 1,000,000 mm and 13,800 × 1,000,000 (mm) = 13.8 × 1,000,000,000 (mm).

3. This distance is approximately the same as that between Paris and Darwin (in north-east Australia) travelling along the smallest arc of the great circle of the Earth and passing through these two cities; 13.8 billion years is the time it would take to travel from one of these cities to the other along this arc at a speed of 1 mm per year.

n) The formation of our planet at around 4,570 km; at that time, gravitational compression also triggered the thermonuclear fusion mechanisms of the hydrogen contained in the solar gas triggering the start of its dazzling light radiation.

o) The birth of our old galaxy at around 10,000 km.

In our Universe where everything moves at stupendous speeds, life on Earth developed in a relatively unobtrusive biosphere i.e. a layer about 10 km thick. Travelling at around 300,000 km/s, light takes less than 2/10ths of a second to travel around our planet; so, one second from the Moon, eight minutes and 30 seconds from the Sun, four years to reach us from its nearest star, and 100,000 years to cross our galaxy [4]. And if we still need to be convinced of the extreme finitude of our biosphere, there are at least 200 billion galaxies in our expanding bubble.

The trajectory of the asteroid (around 10 km of extension) which, when it hit the Earth 66 million years ago, caused the disappearance of the dinosaurs could easily have been slightly modified by a celestial body passing in its vicinity in the solar system. If this had happened then this massive asteroid would not have collided with Earth, homo sapiens would not have emerged and we would not be here to talk about it.

That said, it is obvious that thought in hominids is only a fleeting glimmer, a mere flash of consciousness and civilisation, which will probably be extinguished long before the

---

4. Today, we estimate that our galaxy (the Milky Way) is 100,000 light years across Therefore, although the solar system revolves around the galactic centre at a speed of about 230 km per second, it has only circled the galaxy about 16 times since it came into existence.

Earth still remains in a habitable zone of its giant ageing red Sun (before 500 million years approximately). In the centuries to come, a devastating thermonuclear war is not something we can rule out either. Major natural catastrophes could also occur, such as super-volcano eruptions, massive asteroids colliding into the Earth, pandemics caused by genetically-modified viruses, etc.

Preparing humankind to live on the Moon, Mars or Titan is not a rational response to these possible occurrences. Colonising the Milky Way, as Elon Musk seems to be considering in order to extend the light of consciousness, is pure fantasy! Planets resembling the Earth are probably at least twenty light-years from our Sun. Moreover, because of how life evolves in our biosphere, the functioning of our organisms would not be adapted to these planets.

Let us be absolutely clear, in the meantime a 'less unreasonable' objective would be to use our most advanced and sophisticated techniques with regard to our natural environment, so that in the medium term three to five billion humans could live on Earth in a planetary Garden of Eden and die peacefully and freely when their time comes.

2. Sense and thought

In his book [5], the philosopher Jean-Luc NANCY says:

> Thought weighs exactly the weight of sense. The act of thinking is an effective weighing: the very thought of the world, things, reality as sense... it is the light weight of

---

5. J.-L. NANCY, "The Gravity of Thought, the approach", Ed. La Phocide (Philosophie - d'autre part), Paris, 2008.

an approach bringing us as close as possible to what can not be grasped.

For each meditative thought i.e. one not controlled by reason alone, hovers the elusive scent of its sense, that of which it accounts. Here, we are referring to the very subtle functioning of the brain, a little muddled in its functional ramifications of a certain fuzzy logic; by fuzzy logic we generally mean a logic based on trial and error, more or less random, and generally only retaining what appears to work. It is not dissimilar to the roots of a plant groping for nutrients in the soil.

In regard to thinking, even before pondering sense and thought, a little mental tidy-up may be necessary i.e. rational order or the order of reason.

Is so-called pure reason just a strange anomaly of Nature's fuzzy logic? We might think so. Therefore, to be in a position to give sense and thus create it, it is also occasionally necessary to plunge ourselves into disorder and dreams.

To better understand the statement: "Thought weighs exactly the weight of sense", it is first necessary to define sense and thought.

In the cerebral process of idea formation, we basically distinguish between two phases: the fleeting transitional phase in which a flash synthesis occurs based on a prolific meditative disorder, and a slower stabilisation phase in which this synthesis is refined into a semblance of rational order. We will associate the first phase with the emergence of sense, a highly qualitative leap, and the second with the thought, the expression of that sense.

By plotting the passage of time on a horizontal axis and the weight of sense (its value) on a vertical axis, the resultant graph shows how the formation of an idea resembles a staircase. We can see that thought weighs the true weight of its sense: it is exactly the same height. The first phase which captures the most sensual and most emotional complexity of the idea is not dissimilar to a flash of lightning in a cerebral universe whose centre is everywhere and whose borders are nowhere.

So while we are dreaming, let us enjoy a few words by Michel SERRES [6]:

> Nothing beats a great thought which opens up a grandiose and colourful landscape. The miraculous joy that comes from greater understanding and which turns a humble dwelling into a Mundaneum for anyone who sleeps in a mean lacklustre room. And nothing comes close to an elegant demonstration that adds finesse to reason, an intuition that makes the body fly at the speed of thought that seems even faster than the flash, deep meditation, altitude, slowness, the serene plain of wisdom.

6. M. SERRES, « Les cinq sens », Ed. Grasset, Paris, 1985 ; réédition Ed. Fayard, Paris, 2014.

Point 2

The yawning chasm of the thing-in-itself

Coming back to the Big Bang, talking about spatio-temporal singularity or more precisely quasi-singularity is something that is naturally inaccessible to our understanding. For the ancient Greeks, the beginning of everything was associated with KHAOS, which, in ancient Greek means 'yawning chasm' (hence the notion of 'chaos' in English and French for example). "In the beginning, there was KHAOS," said HESIOD [1]. Yet even today we still wonder what really happened amid the chaos of our Big Bang. It remains a mystery. And as for the thorny issue of the origin of origins, if indeed one even exists, that also remains a mystery. Neither can anybody answer LEIBNIZ' famous question: "Why is there something rather nothing?". We can only consider the existence of a truth in this respect or 'The truth about what the Principle of Being' means.

1. Objects, and their images and representations

As soon as we consider, rightly, that thought is a product of Nature then what this Nature is, its 'thing-in-itself' or

---

1. HESIOD, "Theogony", 115-116.

'Das ding an sich' in the words of KANT [2], it is 'naturally' inaccessible to us. This is of course true for the thing-in-itself of any spatio-temporal subject-part of our world, and sense in particular. From the pre-Socratic philosophers like (for instance) DEMOCRITUS up to our modern-day philosophers, this way of 'seeing' things has gradually become the norm.

In physico-mathematical terms, the same idea can be formulated as follows: the imaging relationship between objects in Nature and the image information we perceive is not invertible. Based on the images (in the broadest meaning) of the object-subject in question, we endeavour to reconstruct it as best we can thus forming, within the meaning of SCHOPENHAUER, acceptable representations of its nature. Even though we can often improve upon these representations, all objects are inevitably obscured from us despite our efforts.

Thus, quantum physics [3] (the physics of extremely small 'objects') marks a departure from what is familiar to us i.e classical physics which describes our everyday environment. The following points in particular challenge our common understanding: the wave behaviour of these objects, the integers and half-integers associated with their quantum states, the superposition of these states, and quantum entanglement [4].

---

2. For example, see KANT'S (translated by TREMESAYGUES and PACAUD), "Critique of Pure Reason", PUF, coll. 'Bibliothèque de Philosophie Contemporaine', 1975, 8e éd., 1975.

3. For more information, read the academic book on the subject by J.-Ph. PÉREZ, R. CARLES, O. PUJOL, « Quantique, fondements et applications », Ed. de Boeck Supérieur, 2013.

4. This is a strange phenomenon where two particles (or groups of particles) form a linked system in which their quantum states depend on each other regardless of the distance between them.

A publication entitled "Nature and the Greeks"[5] by SCHRÖDINGER, a pioneer of quantum mechanics, considers that DEMOCRITUS was perhaps the first thinker to question the sweeping explanation of atomism of that time and his scepticism was long overdue. In fact, he had already realised that is was impossible to close this yawning chasm and all that remained was to confront it with a rigorous and restrained attitude: a combination of the respect due to its longevity and its mobilising ideal produced by the never satisfied desire to fulfil it.

2. Sense and the world

In a chapter of his essays, MONTAIGNE said [6]:

> The world eternally vibrates. All things therein are incessantly moving...Even constancy itself is none other than a slower and more languishing motion. I can not fix my object; 'tis always tottering and reeling by a natural giddiness. I take it as it is at the instant I consider it; the moment I am having fun with it. I do not paint its being. I paint its passage; not a passing from one age to another, or, as the people say, from seven to seven years, but from day to day, from minute to minute.

Four centuries on, quantum physics explains this intuitive perception with more precision. As we shall see in Points 3, 4 and 5, it invites us to think that 'sense' is consubstantial with life. It seems that everything we perceive from

---

5. Lectures given by SCHRÖDINGER at University College, London on 24, 26, 28 and 31 May 1948; translation from English and notes by M. BITBOL and A. BITBOL-HERSPERIES, Ed. Les Belles Lettres, coll. L'Âne d'Or, 2014.
6. M. de MONTAIGNE, Du Repentir – Essai III, 2.

the 'entrails' of the world is related to the quantum world including gravitation and maybe even space. What the physics of these entrails (i.e. that of the extremely small) tells us is that nothing is separable thus dividing the world into separate parts is problematic. What happens at these scales can induce, in a domino effect, important phenomena on larger scales i.e. on the macroscopic scale as well as our own.

Therefore, when we think about life on the surface of our planet, we are referring to reductive representations of the thing in question i.e. its appearance, the role of mutations in its adaptive evolution, homo sapiens and humanity, etc. And it is the same when we ask questions about it: How did it come about? Can it appear otherwise? By dividing these problems into different parts with 'science, prudence and wisdom' (and in terms of space and time), our representations of the world can however be refined a little further; see Point 6 which explores the evolution of these representations.

Our presence in the world should be perceived as being far more complex than a simple face-to-face, or even an element within a whole. This leads us to think of ARAGON when he said: "What would I be without your coming to meet me?". The sense we are talking about here is therefore 'profound' only in that it ultimately emerges from the complexity of each of us in our encounters with others [7] and our interactions with everything that lives in this world.

---

7. Here, 'others' refer to humans in the broadest meaning: the living, as well as those who have left us the living fabric of their memory.

■▼ Point 3

Fundamental representations

A few words about the fundamental representations of our world is an essential prerequisite to any philosophical reflection on Nature and life. It will give us an idea of Universal Gravitation, as well as the Standard Model of elementary particles. To do this, it is necessary to explain the role of mathematics in this respect, a role which is crucial to our vision of the world.

1. Mathematics and Nature

Human intelligence, or at least some form of it, exhibits or constructs so-called abstract structures with regard to others that are less so. These very solid structures constitute the corpus (always in development) of pure mathematics i.e. pure as in the sense of crystals. These structures impose themselves on the humans who formulate and understand them irrespective of their beliefs and what they think about the human sciences for example.

Generally speaking, mathematics makes it possible to construct representations of the physicist's subject-objects. This is particularly true of one branch of mathematics known as algebraic topology. Certain relatively simple topological structures are found in Nature such as fermions, i.e. quarks and electrons, which are the ultimate particles of matter. Their topological structure is rather like a Möbius strip, which is formed by glueing together the ends of a rectangular band after having first performed a half-twist. A fermion of this type is said to have a half-integer spin. Generally, the spin is an internal quantum property of the particles in the same way as an electric charge for example. Regarding this, it is important to note that the concept of the spinor was first exhibited in 1913 by the mathematician Elie CARTAN well before the era of quantum physics and the use of spintronics (spin electronics or magnetoelectronics is a technique that exploits the quantum property of electron spin in order to store data).

As we have briefly illustrated, mathematics play an important role in our representations of the things in our world. To go a little further, let us consider the 'reality' that hides behind the notion of the electron. Due to certain observed phenomena related to what we call in physics, the phenomenon of diffraction [1], it can not be reduced to a particle with mass, an electric charge and a spin. It must also be associated with a wave. Therefore, an electron is partly a wave and a partly a particle. This is known as wave–particle duality.

SCHRÖDINGER's equation, the cornerstone of quantum mechanics, takes into account this wave aspect. It is a differential equation [2] like many others and one which can be resolved with a computer. For example, by resolving this equation for the benzene molecule [3], we get a probabilistic

---

1. To learn more, visit: https://www.futura-sciences.com/sciences/definitions/physique-diffraction-1019/
2. To learn more, visit: https://www.cmath.fr/bac+1/equationdifferentielle/cours.php

representation of the electronic distribution of this molecule, although the position of its electrons can not be further specified. In particular, this equation allows us to understand the mechanisms of image formation in high-resolution electron microscopy [4]. This is how we visualise structures at the atomic level. Biochemists have integrated these representations into life sciences and progressing towards genetics for over 50 years. This is already upsetting our vision of humanity, and consequently psychology and sociology.

In mathematics, a problem is said to be ill-conditioned if a small variation in the data or the initial conditions can cause its solution to vary in a very significant manner. Beyond a certain spatial and temporal threshold, the equations that govern most of Nature's phenomena are ill-conditioned. To 'standardise' their solutions, it is necessary to introduce certain constraints or change the scale. For example, for problems of image reconstruction in electron microscopy or astronomy, spatial and angular resolving thresholds must be introduced. To give you a better idea, in electron microscopy this resolving threshold is approximately one tenth of a nanometre (NB: a nanometre is a billionth of a metre or a millionth of a millimetre). In other words, we can only restore the object on a scale that is higher than a tenth of a nanometre.

The moral of this story (or its philosophy) is that we can only 'decipher the word' at a certain level of resolution, which varies depending on the questions we ask. So, to return to humanity, while it is impossible to predict the

---

3. To learn more, visit: https://fr.wikipedia.org/wiki/Benz%C3%A8ne
4. Consult the book by: A. Lannes, J.-Ph. Pérez, « Optique de Fourier en microscopie électronique », Masson, Paris, 1983.

behaviour of an individual in the short term, it may be possible to understand that of a community in the medium term e.g. through its demographic evolution. A rather strange paradox, isn't it?

2. Fundamental interactions

In our world, the one which resulted from our Big Bang [5], all the physical, chemical and biological processes we know can be analysed with the help of four so-called fundamental interactions i.e. gravitational, electromagnetic, and weak and strong nuclear interactions. Touching upon their nature, we can present them in the following manner.

Gravitational interaction takes into account the way bodies are attracted to one another owing to their mass. In fact, given the Einsteinian concepts introduced in the next section, this is not an interaction within the strict meaning of the term. Nevertheless, as an initial approximation, we can describe the relative movement of these bodies by applying Newtonian physics i.e. by considering that a certain 'gravitational force' is exerted between them [6].

Electromagnetic interaction takes into account the way bodies are attracted to and repel one another owing to their charge. This interaction is involved in all electric and

---

5. A 'chaotic' event such as a Big Bang would not necessarily create a world like ours. In principle, another Big Bang could give rise to a different set of interactions, and even (why not?) a world that would be better than ours, a world for example where violence would not be consubstantial with life (see point 7). If this somewhat fanciful (let's face it) conjecture turned out to be true then our world would not be at the height of all the power of Being; see the foreword of this essay.

6. For more details about this point, consult the academic book by: J.-Ph. Pérez, O. Pujol, « Mécanique : fondements et application », Chap. 12, Ed. Dunod, 7e édition, 2014.

magnetic phenomena and especially in everything related to light, chemistry and molecular and cellular biology, so basically all living things.

The weak nuclear interaction is associated with certain radioactivity phenomena that govern life in our biosphere. In particular, this interaction triggers the process of nuclear fusion in the stars and the Sun. It also occurs in the processes that maintain magma in a state of fusion beneath the Earth's crust and especially plate tectonics and volcanism.

The strong nuclear interaction structures matter in the sense that it is involved in the cohesion of atomic nuclei. Strong nuclear fusion reactions, the source of stars' energy, also arise from this fundamental interaction.

The theory which describes gravitation is known as the theory of General Relativity while the theory used to define the three others is known as the Standard Model. It is used to model the world of elementary quantum particles in terms of their identities and interactions. We will now give a brief overview of these theoretical representations.

3. General Relativity

In the theory of general relativity formulated by EINSTEIN in 1915, everything happens as if the spacetime of our Universe was a gelatinous substance; a relatively elastic fabric woven via unidentified quantum particles. Since our Big Bang, this 'jelly' has been expanding. Time passes 'locally' more or less quickly depending on the local geometry of this invisible fabric. In turn this geometry depends on the mass of objects that are moved or carried there [7]. The presence of massive objects significantly modifies the local geometry of this space fabric. Particles free of any interaction move along the geodesics [8] of this geometry. In this space, the speed of any object is at most equal to EINSTEIN's constant c; this constant is the speed of light in a vacuum i.e. around 300,000 km/s.

Techniques that are widely used today rely on these phenomena. For example, Global Navigation Satellite Systems (GNSS) based on a constellation of satellites known as GPS (in the USA), GLONASS in the Russian Federation and GALILEO (in the European Union) are sensitive to two relativistic effects; the first being special relativity and the second, and most important, being general relativity. General relativity is linked to the Earth's 'mass presence': it is around six times greater than special relativity which, due to the movement of the satellite, has the effect of slowing down clocks. It is therefore the speeding up of atomic clocks on board the satellites that prevails. Due to their distance from the terrestrial geoid (20,000 km approx.), these clocks vibrate faster than those on the Earth. To ensure temporal accuracy, this must be taken into account. In fact, in these positioning

---

7. For related scientific information, see the new presentation of EINSTEIN's fundamental contribution: "La théorie de la relativité restreinte et générale", collection *IDEM*, Ed. Dunod, 2012.

8. Einstein's spacetime is a space in which physical considerations make it possible to define 'locally' a distance between its points. In this spacetime, a path between two points, A and B, is said to be optimal if its length is 'locally minimal': an infinitesimal variation in this path increases its length. The A—B 'geodetic' is the optimal path between A and B, or one of the optimal paths if there are several. For example, on a surface (more or less spherical) such as the Earth where the distances are those we can measure on its surface, the Paris—Beijing geodetic is the smallest arc of the great circle of the earth passing through these two cities.

systems, networks of receivers on the ground and users' receivers, pick up the signals transmitted by these satellite constellations along with time lags, which can be measured very accurately. Once the relativistic effects and other effects linked to the crossing of the atmosphere have been corrected, the greater the distances travelled, the greater these lags are. Since we know the position of satellites along their respective trajectories, we can accurately calculate the position of the receivers on the ground.

4. The Standard Model

As previously indicated, fermions – quarks and electrons (notably) – are ultimate particles of matter. They have an odd half integer spin. Bosons, which have a 1 or 0 spin, are the particles involved in the fundamental interactions of our world as they are modelled today. For example, photons are the bosons of the electromagnetic interaction while gluons are the bosons of the strong interaction.

The H boson [9], with spin zero, was first proposed in 1964 and was confirmed in 2012 through experiments. The mass of a fermion accounts for the opposition of the H bosons or, more precisely, the 'H field' in terms of setting in motion the fermion in question; the stronger the opposition, the greater the mass.

---

9. This boson is often called the 'Higgs Boson'. In fact, ENGLERT and BROUT had already conceptualised it six months before HIGGS did so independently. The researchers behind this 'conceptual discovery' won the Nobel Prize in Physics in 2013; BROUT did not attend having died in 2011. ENGLERT and HIGGS finally agreed to call this particle the 'H boson'.

Immediately after the Big Bang, the H field did not exist. When the Universe started cooling and its temperature dropped below a critical threshold, this field 'spontaneously' appeared; all the particles sensitive to it thus acquired a mass. For example, quarks and electrons each have their own mass while photons and gluons are massless.

In the 1970s, physicists realised that the electromagnetic interaction and the weak interaction were in fact manifestations of the same interaction i.e. the electroweak interaction. This unification is the basis of the Standard Model. Photons and W and Z bosons are particles of this interaction; W and Z bosons (unlike photons and gluons) have an appreciable mass.

The energy of our world is essentially confined within the atomic nuclei. These tiny regions, relative to the size of the atoms, are governed by the strong interaction. The manner in which quarks are confined there via gluons is known as 'quantum chromodynamics' in the Standard Model. Virtual colours are associated with the quantum numbers of 'objects' in this world, hence the employed terminology.

When these nuclei are disrupted (we will see how Nature does this in Point 4), the extreme energy released as a result is the epitome of violence itself. Atomic nuclei are thus where the world is robustly anchored, essential but redoubtable in view of life.

As previously mentioned, visible and invisible light waves, and the appearance and evolution of life is actually an electromagnetic interaction. In the Standard Model, following on from the fundamental contributions of DIRAC and FEYNMAN (formulated between around 1930 and 1950), this interaction is described in the formal framework of what we call quantum electrodynamics. While the field of action of weak and strong nuclear interactions is very localised, the field of the electromagnetic interaction is extremely wide. Electromagnetic violence certainly exists, one only has to consider lightning or chemical bombs, but it is negligible compared to that of the strong interaction.

Generally speaking, Nature seems to have adopted very specific mathematical structures for the various types of quantum phenomena in our world. Those involved in the Standard Model fall into certain 'special unitary groups' [10]. Yet why these, which are already very elaborate, and not others which are even more complex? Would they be more 'stable' in a sense that has yet to be defined?

What we should take away from this state of affairs is that everything that touches on the complexity of things in our biosphere is fragile, and is all the more fragile when it touches on the sublime nature of quantum electrodynamics; let us dare to say it: consciousness, spirituality, love (in the sense of *agapê*), fraternity, poetry, art and knowledge. If you are in need of further proof, simply consider the damage created by the thermonuclear bombs dropped on Hiroshima and Nagasaki.

Before delving further (in Point 5) into the texture of living things, there is a prerequisite that is far from human i.e. atomic transmutations behind the famous stardust of which we are made. The title of the following point describes, in this respect, processes that are far from gentle.

---

10. Whether you are a mathematician or a seeker of truth, take a look at these exciting course notes: https://www.math.u-psud.fr/~paulin/notescours/cours_centrale.pdf . Also, see the reference on https://fr.wikipedia.org/wiki/Groupe about special unitary groups.

In the cosmic forges of gravitation

Once upon a time there was a day, or rather a clear night, when one of our ancestors started to wonder about all those little lights shimmering in the firmament. He must have been the first hominid to have his head in the stars. But where, when and under what circumstances? Was he worried or reassured? Nobody knows and who cares! We had to wait to until the twentieth century to even begin to understand how life was forged, and is being forged now and forever in the skies of our Universe. In this cosmic laboratory, today's astrophysicists tell us that many other things are being made, strange dynamic structures that the gods of yesteryear and today hardly even care about.

Before we speak of life, let us take a step back from all Nature's achievements. This is the main objective of this crucial scientific and philosophical point.

1. The remnants of supernovae

In the end-of-life explosion of a star eight to twelve times bigger than our Sun the dust that populates our Universe is formed. An event of this type i.e. what we call a *supernova* is relatively rare with on average two per century in a galaxy such as ours. That is about one every two or three seconds in the observable Universe i.e. in its vastness! Under certain conditions and in accordance with hypothetical procedures, a very small amount of this star dust can organise itself into cells of primitive life several billion years later.

A *supernova* event results from the gravitational collapse of the iron core that formed in the heart of a star of this type in its end-of-life phase. This iron is in fact the ultimate product of the thermonuclear fusion cycles occurring inside the star in this phase of its life. The majority of the atoms that we know form in a domino effect from hydrogen: thus in the centre there is iron and then silicon, oxygen, neon, carbon, helium and the remaining hydrogen as we move towards the periphery of the star.

Weak and strong nuclear interactions are involved in the diverse and complex mechanisms of a star's life. The fusion of atomic nuclei is generally accompanied by a considerable release of energy. If gravitation did not keep the entire star under incredible pressure, its lifespan would be very short much like that of a thermonuclear bomb.

When the mass of the iron heart of a star (*supernova*) reaches a critical value i.e. in the region of about 1.4 times that of the Sun, the gravitational pressure causes this heart to collapse in on itself. The iron is transformed into a material essentially composed of neutrons (electrically neutral particles). When the density of this neutron matter attains another critical value, the repulsive forces of this strong interaction prevent this collision. The matter which falls onto this internal part, measuring a few kilometres in diameter, can no longer compress it and it bounces off the hard neutron core creating a shock that spreads out towards the periphery. The ensuing explosion disperses (into space) the famous star dust created in earlier thermonuclear fusion cycles.

From these *supernova* remains, stars and their associated planetary systems will be born in less tumultuous moments. These *supernova* remains collect stray hydrogen and the already highly-processed dust. In the gestation period of several million years preceding the birth of one of these new stars, once again it is the gravitational interaction that dominates. The hydrogen in these planetary nebulae is compressed until it triggers the thermonuclear processes. This is when the stars light up and illuminate their planetary systems often for several billion years.

2. The emergence of life

In outer space, on the surface of planets similar to our own, things end up by calming down, more or less, as the atoms collide less violently. The frequency of these encounters is reflected in the temperature with some accuracy thus the higher the frequency of these encounters, the higher the temperature. In this state of permanent agitation, certain atoms ignore each other as they have no natural affinity, while others are attracted to each other owing to their strong chemical affinities. These potentialities for union are the basis of quantum electrodynamics. In brief, the phase in which the photons involved in the electromagnetic interaction take part in a crazy quantum dance giving rise to the first cells of life, here and there, in the Universe. How exactly and under what conditions does this occur? Nobody knows! It is an enigma but it is not a complete mystery. Conducting fundamental research in this domain (see footnote 5, Point 5) seems far wiser than attempting to send a crew of astronauts to Mars.

That life exists elsewhere in our galaxy will probably be confirmed in the medium term by spectral signatures (infrared) of water, carbon dioxide, methane and ozone found in the atmosphere of such and such exoplanet. As these exoplanets are probably around more than twenty light-years from the Earth, sending a space probe crammed with artificial intelligence to inquire whether this is the case seems unreasonable [1]. For example, at a cruising speed of 300 km/s, the journey, which would be incredibly energy-consuming and perilous, would take more than 20,000 years (or more than 200 years at 30,000 km/s).

3. White dwarves, neutron stars and black holes

Stars whose mass is lower than around eight times that of our Sun end their lives as white dwarves. Those whose mass is higher, but around twelve times lower than that of our Sun, explode and become *supernovae* ending their lives as neutron stars with a residual mass of around one to three times that of our Sun. Finally, those whose mass is even greater end their lives as black holes; a celestial body is designated thus as any light emitted within it can not escape. The luminosity of a black hole (which is therefore zero) is lower than that of a neutron star, which is even lower than

---

1. In fact, we are expressing our reaction to "L'odyssée interstellaire" (The interstellar odyssey) by Vincent AMOUROUX and Alex BARRY, a compelling documentary of 208 minutes.

that of a white dwarf. The density of white dwarf matter is lower than that of a neutron star, which in turn is even lower than that of a black hole.

Let us look at what a neutron star actually is. As indicated above, a neutron star is what remains of a star eight to twelve times bigger than our Sun after it has exploded and dispersed (into our Universe) the cosmic dust of which we are all made. So, what remains of this star that was so powerful and majestic in its prime? Well, a compact rather dark matter almost entirely composed of neutrons packed (by gravitation) into a sphere measuring around twenty kilometres in diameter. Therefore, it is very dense compared to the Earth and living organisms. In the internal core of a star of this type, the volumic mass is in the region of one million tonnes per cubic millimetre, while the volumic mass of water, for example, is only one milligram per cubic millimetre [2]. In our biosphere, the nuclei of dense matter, the nuclei of atoms, are far apart from each other relative to their size.

Now, let us see how physicists represent the tiny physical object they call a neutron. To give you an idea of the size of this particle imagine that an atom, which is around a tenth of nanometre, was increased to the size of a football pitch i.e. 100 metres; the size of a neutron would then be around a millimetre.

In terms of its quantum entity, a neutron has three quarks. These quarks have a mass and an electrical charge, which takes into account their capacity to interact with other electrically charged bodies. Two of them, which have the

---

2. By definition, the density of a body is the ratio between its volumic mass and that of water. In the heart of a neutron star, the density is around 10^{15} (a million billion). Indeed, a million tonnes is 10^9 kg, i.e. 10^{12}g, and therefore 10^{15} mg.

same small charge of -e/3 (a third of the charge of an electron), repel each other while the third which has a charge of 2e/3 (opposite to the sum of the two other charges) is attracted by the latter. A neutron is electrically neutrally, hence its name [3]. Inside the neutron, these three quarks repel and attract each other electrically via photons, although they attract each other more strongly via gluons.

But what are all these quarks, photons, gluons and other ultimate particles in the world made of? Even our most eminent physicists can only describe the phenomena in terms of their presence. That said, although these particles are elusive, scientists can use them in experiments and even calculate their mass [4].

4. Fusion of neutron stars

The story of the fusion of two neutron stars detected on 17 August 2017 could be told like this. Around 130 million years ago in a galaxy far far away, two neutron stars hurtled towards each other through Einstein's gelatinous spacetime fabric. This fabric was affected locally by their presence thus affecting the dynamics of their encounter. The gravitational waves emitted propagated in this jelly at the speed of light in a vacuum.

---

3. A proton has three quarks but its charge is e as opposed to that of an electron. Two of these quarks have a charge of 2e/3 while the third has a charge of -e/3. In our world, the proton is an important particle as its quarks, photons and gluons comprise the nucleus of a hydrogen atom.

4. To learn more, visit: https:www.pourlascience.fr/sd/physique/proton-et-neutron-une-difference-de-masse-enfin-expliquee-par-le-calcul-12083.php

In the fractions of a second preceding the collision of our two stars, the speed of one relative to the other was around 100,000 km/s. Moreover, both of these stars were rotating and deforming at speeds of up to 200,000 km/s on the ground. Furthermore, their direction of rotation may have differed. In fact, we do not precisely know the impact speeds of the neutrons of one in terms of their initial impact on partner neutrons of the other, but they were probably close to the speed of light. In these gigantic cosmic forges of gravitation, the prodigious nucleosynthesis reactions that ensued could then begin. An extremely bright cosmic flash signalled the end of the critical phase of these fantastic reactions. A spectrum analysis of this flash in the visible and infrared spectra, and the light that followed for two days (turning from blue to red), gave an idea of the quantity of heavy and rare metals created during this cosmic nucleosynthesis: a mass of about 16,000 times that of the Earth's including ten times the Earth's gold and platinum!

The gravitational waves generated by the energy of this fusion reached Earth after 130 million years, slightly affecting the distances between points in our local space. It was these variations in lengths lasting a hundred seconds that were detected by the ultra-sensitive interferometers in Virgo and Ligo [5]. These experimental systems are located very far from each other with one in Italy (Virgo) and two (Ligo) in states far from one another in the USA.

---

5. See for example: http://www.cnrs.fr/publications/imagesdelaphysique/couv-PDF/IdP2010/03_Virgo_Laser.pdf

■ Point 5

The constructive processes of quantum biology

Today, we still have a long way to go in terms of understanding the myriad potentialities of the quantum electrodynamics of life. Certain traditional approaches, such as those found in Chinese or African medicine, can prove to be more effective than others that are, *a priori*, part of a conventional scientific approach. Naturally, it would be necessary to research the 'active ingredients' of the remedies used, and analyse the electromagnetic processes involved in some of these practices. In particular, we are referring to hypnosis, acupuncture and osteopathy, as well as the relative effectiveness of some alternative medicines. Obvious clinical symptoms (e.g. burns) can also heal rapidly following treatment from certain traditional healers thus giving us food for thought in terms of these strange phenomena. However, at first glance only one thing is clear, we would need to investigate what happens at the various scales where these phenomena occur and this would involve very complex basic research.

For example, it is said that the biological environment (warm and moist) is not conducive to preserving the quantum coherence of the particles which comprise it i.e. their wave-particle duality. This quantum incoherence becomes even more pronounced when we observe living organisms at scales greater than one micron (i.e. one thousandth of a millimetre). In fact, what we find is quite different from what we find at scales of (or less than) a few nanometres. Yet these are the very size scales of the macromolecules involved in cellular life.

It would appear that quantum biology is a reality we are only just beginning to explore. Two articles on a series of experiments illustrate these findings. The experiments concern the chlorophyll function in plant cells and vibrations in the microtubules of cervical neurons which, it is thought, are likely to play a role in the emergence of consciousness. The publications in question analyse the quantum mechanisms that might be involved in these processes.

However, in terms of scientific representations of our world, life is studied within the framework of biology, which is fundamentally analysed through organic chemistry; this chemistry is ultimately analysed at the nanometric level through quantum physics. In our approach to what life is, these reduction processes are, naturally, not invertible. Quantum instabilities can thus sometimes induce unexpected phenomena at the various scales of living organisms.

Before reading the next two sections, the reader is invited to refer to a paper entitled 'Quantum biology revisited' [1]. The main results of this recent paper are as follows: Nature, instead of trying to avoid quantum incoherence and dissipation, exploits them via certain 'group interactions' (exciton-bath interactions) in order to create efficient energy flows. The efficiency of these energy transfer processes practically

---

1. J. Cao, R.J. Cogdell, D.F. Coke, and many others, "Quantum biology revisited", Sciences Advances, Vol 6, N° 14, Apr 2020, eaaz4888 DOI: 10.1126/sciadv.aaz4888.

equates to that of the corresponding coherent quantum systems thus leading to possible misinterpretations. In any case, concepts related to quantum biology can be very useful for gaining deeper and clearer insights into the quantum physics of larger systems.

1. The quantum world of the chlorophyll function

The process by which plant cells capture and convert light to produce the organic molecules they require seems to have no equivalent in classical physics.

The macromolecules responsible for performing this role are composed of chromophores attached to proteins in the cell. These chromophores give plants their distinctive green colouring and it is within them that the initial phase of photosynthesis takes place. These chromophores capture photons from sunlight before transferring their energy to the rest of the cell.

Researchers believe they have identified the quantum processes responsible for the efficiency of this function[2], which is approximately 95%. Based on their findings, it was found that the vibrations of the chromophores involved in energy transfer could not occur classically and that their efficiency appears to rely on quantum mechanisms which, as we will see later, would have to be highly 'fraternal'.

---

2. O'REILLY EJ, OLAYA-CASTRO A, "Non-classicality of the molecular vibrations assisting exciton energy transfer at room temperature." Nature Communications, 2014, DOI: 10.1038/ncomms4012 (open access).

Molecular vibrations are caused by the periodic movements of atoms in a molecule. When two chromophores vibrate in phase i.e. 'together', a resonance is created thus making it possible for efficient energy exchanges to take place. Under certain conditions (as set out in the researchers' article of footnote 2), discrete units of energy, energy *quanta*, are exchanged at room temperature in a very short period of time, less than one thousandth of a billionth of a second.

Does this process fall within the realm of classical physics? The researchers have demonstrated that it is not the case. Chromophores can only be identified in terms of their position and velocity in a probabilistic or collective manner rendering individual predictions impossible. Therefore, it must be a quantum mechanism corresponding to a coherent exchange of quantum energy. A superposition of quantum states is established between excitation and energy transfer within the chromophore.

Other quantum processes of this type have been identified, such as structural changes in the chromophores associated with vision when photons are absorbed, or the recognition of one protein by another during olfaction.

The proposed theories are highly complex. However, what we can take away is that the origin and understanding of biological organisms is a matter of quantum electrodynamics. This also supports the following idea that as soon as certain conditions are met, life can appear in our Universe. These conditions are not necessarily those currently found in our biosphere nor those found, for example, in Icelandic hot springs 3,500 metres below the ocean.

2. At the quantum core of cervical functions

In the late twentieth century, the anaesthetist Stuart HAMEROFF and the mathematician Roger PENROSE, presented a hypothesis in which the "production" of consciousness, whose nature and origin remains largely unknown, "derives" from processes occurring deep within the cervical neurons; also involved are microtubules, the fibres that make up the cytoskeleton and other filaments.

Like the discovery of quantum vibrations in chromophores (whose neurons are clearly devoid of them), Japanese researchers, and others later, came to the conclusion that similar phenomena occur at the level of neuronal microtubules.

The authors of the related articles suggest that brain waves, long identified using electroencephalographic techniques, are produced by deep vibrations at the microtubule level. Other researchers suggest that anaesthesia, which removes consciousness without paralysing other brain activity, also alters the activity of the microtubules.

For HAMEROFF and PENROSE [3], it would now be clear that quantum vibrations in microtubules are directly involved in neuronal and synaptic functions. These quantum vibrations would connect the brain to preconscious self-organising processes that would constitute, in depth, the 'quantum reality' of consciousness [4].

---

3. HAMEROFF S, PENROSE R, "Consciousness in the universe: a review of the 'Orch OR' theory", Physics of Life Review, Aug 20, 2013.

4. In this paragraph, the use of the conditional tense is required as everything depends on what we mean by 'consciousness'.

3. The quantum universe of genetics and epigenetics

The term 'epigenetics' comes from the ancient Greek; *épi* meaning 'above' and genetics. This field of biology studies the molecular mechanisms that modulate the expression of genetic heritage according to context.

While genetics is a science that studies heredity and genes, epigenetics is concerned with a layer of additional information that tells us how these genes will be used (or not) by a cell. It is an analysis of living organisms that partially belies the tyranny or fatality of genes. In terms of evolution, epigenetics help us to explain how the functional specificities of life are acquired i.e. are passed on from one generation to the next, or are lost once inherited. What this means in practice is that our behaviours and interactions with the outside environment influence our genes.

Today, it is widely known that genetic information is carried by deoxyribonucleic acid (DNA), a macromolecule formed by the sequencing of numerous nucleotides [5]. The DNA molecule comprises two chains of nucleotides wound in a double helix. It is the sequence or order and number of nucleotides in a gene that carries the genetic information.

DNA is notably involved in the synthesis of proteins via messenger ribonucleic acid (mRNA). Without going into detail about the related mechanisms, it is understood that

---

5. A nucleotide consists of a phosphate group, glucide (deoxyribose) and a nitrogen-containing base. There are four different nitrogen-containing bases i.e. adenine, cytosine, guanine and thymine. In DNA, nucleotides come in pairs. Therefore, opposite cytosine we always find guanine and opposite adenine we always find thymine.

during evolution everything occurs at the nanoscale scale of quantum biology [6].

The mechanisms of epigenetics, in particular, are thus related to quantum electrodynamics as they occur via a chemical modification of the DNA called methylation: CH_3 radicals called methyls (a carbon atom bonded to three hydrogen atoms) latch onto the DNA via a single electron from the carbon atom that seeks to pair with an available electron on the DNA thus forming a chemical bond with it.

4. From quantum affinities to conscious fraternities

As indicated in Point 4, fundamental quantum affinities are at the origin of the first 'living dynamic system' i.e. an open biological system capable of transforming the energy it receives into a certain local dynamic order that can diversify but only at the cost of its more or less programmed death.

These quantum processes occur, in a very intimate and profound way, in the teeming complexity of dynamic life systems that have evolved into a wild firework display over more than three billion years. At the nanoscale level, it is these mechanisms which oppose the unstoppable increase in the entropy [7] of living organisms i.e. the inevitable race towards the dust they will become after death.

---

6. According to recent research following the discovery of a model of the molecular structure of ribose (a sugar) in a meteorite billions of years old, some scientists now believe that RNA evolved before DNA in the process of life formation.

7. Entropy is a quantity which characterises the degree of disorder or disorganisation in a physical system. As a system becomes disorganised, its entropy increases.

We started from the premise that life appeared and developed in a bath of fermions and photons by exploiting the potential of electromagnetic interactions of the atoms of hydrogen, carbon, oxygen, nitrogen, etc., in other words, from the constituents of the dust left over from *supernovae*. These potentialities are practically infinite; this means, *ipso-facto*, we are not able to understand in detail how we transition from the quantum nanometric world to the first cells of life, let alone to the primates we are today. At best we can model certain more or less identifiable links in the chain, albeit taking a reductive and systemic approach.

What we have just mentioned occurs in life at all scales i.e. from molecular biology through to the complexity of our human societies including all the key evolution stages of living systems. In this respect, quantum affinities participate in life rather like light. Just as some light is visible and some is not, it can also be said that within the very broad spectrum [8] of affinities some are conscious and some are not, and this is probably occurring within us all. What this means is that certain quantum affinities which soothe our unconscious mind by creating this or that drug 'fraternise' with others that structure and animate the conscious part. Perhaps this is one of the reasons why some people are optimistic and others are less so.

The transition from unconscious affinities in the nanoscale world to the more conscious affinities seen in some animals and especially humans is not well understood. However, this does not mean we should not try to understand what can be understood, or indeed do away with reason or

---

8. Here, the meaning of 'spectrum' is that used in physics e.g. the spectrum of sunlight with the different colours of a rainbow.

take refuge in a holistic vision of the world i.e. a globalist vision such as the neo-Gnostic mysticism discussed in the work entitled "La mystique néo-gnostique" by Jean-Émile CHARON [9]. It is precisely because the determinism and positivism of the early twentieth century are no longer scientifically acceptable, as everything is ultimately quantum and hence ultimately probabilistic, that we are currently witnessing a return of religious beliefs and the emergence of neo-Gnostic conceptions of this nature.

So, what does reason tell us about our observations of the world? Well, if we consider Nature's myriad audacious achievements some are beautiful, good and sublime while others are downright awful! Therefore, if certain types of thinking, behaviour or development fail then others will take over. In other words, Nature's fuzzy logic eliminates what does not work when necessary. Thus, what seems to prevail today, such as human consciousness in particular, could one day – if we are not careful – disappear altogether. The book by the naturalist and philosopher, Yves PACCALET, entitled "L'humanité disparaîtra, bon débarras !" [10] (Humankind will disappear, good riddance!) has a much to say on this subject.

---

9. Based on this doctrine, the 'Spirit' would dwell in every electron in our world. The book in which J.-E. CHARON presents this vision entitled 'Le Monde Eternel des Éons' was first published by Editions Stock in 1980.

10. Y. PACCALET, "L'humanité disparaîtra, bon débarras ! ", Ed. J'ai lu, 2007.

◤ Point 6

The evolution of representations

Over the course of civilisation, our representations of the things in our world have changed. For example, in the Mediterranean world the Greek philosopher ANAXAGORAS suggested (500 B.C.E.) that the Sun was a massive 'red-hot stone' located far from the Earth [1]. He estimated its radius to be around 60 km while it is around 696,000 km. Challenging the commonly-held beliefs of the time resulted in his exile from Athens. It was then necessary to wait until 1543 for COPERNICUS to put forward a reasonably acceptable model of the Universe in which the Sun is at its centre with the planets orbiting around it.

Today, it is common knowledge that the Earth viewed from Saturn is a tiny 'blue pixel' which would completely disappear from sight as soon as we were in the vicinity of *Proxima Centauri* (our nearest star around four light-years away). In that far distant sky, our Sun would be clearly visible but would be one star among many. Finally, the size of our galaxy is approximately 100,000 light-years but if we managed to reach the heart of Andromeda (the nearest spiral

---

1. For ANAXAGORAS, the Sun was an igneous stone; see "Les présocratiques", Bibliothèque de la Pléiade, ANAXAGORE A3, A11, A12, and for information about his measurement miscalculations see: www.jf-noblet.fr/grecs/anaxagore.pdf.

galaxy located 2.55 million light-years away), we would have to be an expert astronomer to point out our galaxy.

As for the representations of the world expressed in founding texts such as the Book of Genesis in the Torah and those of the late twentieth century, the changes are profound. Our vision of the world and life in particular has changed enormously. While many of today's Christians believe in a possible creation, they no longer kill each other because they want to know whether it was god or the devil who created the world [2]. However, it is worth noting that in the United States, 46% of the total population are dyed-in-the-wool creationists who believe that god created the Earth and humankind as we know it 10,000 years ago, including the vice-president of the 'Dis-united States': Mike Pence!

1. Simplistic representations and their ideologies

Our beliefs (or convictions) are often overly simplistic representations of the world and, whether religious or economic, they are also potentially tragic. Our history is sadly rife with them and any education worth its salt should systematically address this. These representations are associated

---

2. The two opposing principles i.e. good vs. evil (being vs. nothingness), passing for 'duality', is often mistakenly attributed to ancient Manichaeism whereas Being is 'Everything' and nothingness is 'nothing'. This opposition, based on so-called 'Cathar' beliefs, is taken to the extreme here; by creating a world in which it is manure that makes vegetables grow, evil (Satan) has broken the chain of Good (god). However, medieval Catholics believed that by creating the world, god is good and perfect while evil is a simple 'lack of goodness'. In the Middle Ages, the armed wing of the Roman Catholic Church subjected the Cathars to ordeal by fire (for a range of reasons including political ones) systematically exterminating them.

with received ideas and while intended to be fair and profound they in no way reflect what living organisms really are in terms of how they have evolved in our biosphere. The two following examples serve to illustrate this:

1) The voluntary termination of a pregnancy and euthanasia must be prohibited in law in all circumstances because life is a gift from god [3].

2) The more numerous we are, the stronger we are. Therefore, ever more ambitious uncurtailed growth is required to create more jobs [4].

In fact, the obscure nature of statements of this type is far more concerning than global warming and is, in fact, one of its driving factors. A scourge on humanity!

Yet who dares speak out? The UNITED NATIONS, the IMF or POPE FRANCIS in his encyclical on the environment and human ecology entitled *Laudato Si* (Praise be to Thee)? Certainly not! This work does not even question the first injunction of the patriarchal verse 28 in chapter one of the Book of Genesis in which, having created man and woman, god blesses Adam and Eve saying:

"And you, be fruitful and multiply, increase greatly on the earth and multiply in it."

---

3. "Life is a gift from god" is a statement that conforms to the ideological corpus of the Roman Catholic Church and many other religions; it is also a common theme of POPE FRANCIS. Based on the analysis of SPINOZA in the appendix to his first book on Ethics, "the will of god" that gave us life is the "asylum of ignorance".

4. The validity of certain analyses put forward by economic and social sciences depends on the way in which the chosen parameters are taken into account when modelling the problems under consideration. As for many of Nature's other phenomena, long-term forecasts obtained in this way are rarely stable and hence are not reliable. That said, one can not attribute such simplistic inferences to these branches of science.

We are entitled to ask the question: who is the wisest? POPE FRANCIS or CIORAN when he said [5]:

> "Nothing better illustrates to what extent humanity is regressing than the impossibility of finding a single group or tribe where birth still provokes mourning and lamentation."

Not one! That said, there is surely a happy medium somewhere [6]. Yet are we responsible for the worrying population growth in Africa and India, for example? Perhaps, a little but in an in-depth reflection on 'Living Together', we must necessarily define its contours sometimes even fixing limits and boundaries. In this context, it is necessary to support (globally) those who are trying to reduce the influence of ideologies that wish to boost the birth rate.

And as for politicians, either through ignorance or vested interests, they often only scratch the surface of the complexity of societal problems. Due to the risk of being termed divisive (so they say), they rarely specify in detail which representations of the world they base their views on. They simply talk about the values of civilisation as if that were enough, which is far from satisfactory.

For example, so-called universal values, such as the right to vote, are not appropriate in countries where religions encourage their followers to have as many children as possible [7]. The influence of the laity is thus diminished.

---

5. E. Cioran, « De l'inconvénient d'être né », Ed. Gallimard, 1987.

6. The growth of the global population is such that in 2020 we can already call it overpopulation. Ecological overpopulation is at around 70%. A reasonable goal for the planet would be to have about five billion people by 2050 rather than ten. Globally, we must encourage women not to have children or to have one or two at most; some women have already taken this decision.

This is the case for the laity in Palestine who must coexist cheek by jowl with the ultra-orthodox Jews in Jerusalem, and the Sunni and Shiite Muslims living in the Gaza Strip and the West Bank. In this context, democracy is accelerating the detonation of these demographic time bombs, which are already threatening to explode at any moment due to the ongoing conflict.

Serious secularists seek to control fertility, aware of the economic and environmental impact on their country and the wider world. Therefore, they are more clear-sighted and responsible.

In our view, the simple fact of being born should not automatically entitle individuals to vote at an age defined by law (the so-called age of reason); potential voters should be required to demonstrate this reason; naturally, all these potential voters could vote for setting up the commissions of wise individuals tasked with judging this.

2. A hierarchy of representations but which one?

As indicated in Point 2, the object-image relationship in terms of mathematics and philosophy is not invertible. For modern physicists, representations of the same inevitably incomplete object-subject are nevertheless hierarchical.

---

7. In some religions having their roots in Greek antiquity, 'woman' is identified with the land while 'man' is the ploughman; social welfare for the elderly was thus guaranteed by having a large number of children.

To clarify what we mean here by hierarchy, refer to what PAULI [8] had to say on the subject:

> "It appears that as physics continues to evolve, it does not dismiss its earlier stages as null and void but rather confines itself to delimiting their scope of application by integrating them into wider systems as 'special cases'."

For example, let us consider the theory of special relativity formulated by EINSTEIN in 1905. This theory, which builds on work carried out in the late nineteenth century by LORENTZ and Henri POINCARÉ, draws all its physical conclusions from the fact that the speed of light in a vacuum has the same value in all inertial frames of reference [9]; these frames of reference differ only in their constant relative travelling speed. The corresponding equations known as the LORENTZ transformations produce forecasts that often fly in the face of common sense yet none of them have been disproved by experiments. This approach was modified by EINSTEIN in 1915 in order to take into account gravitation, hence special relativity became general (see section 3 of Point 3 and section 4 of Point 4).

Between 1926 and 1927, DIRAC was not satisfied with the relativistic equation that took into account (at that time) the wave mechanics of very fast electrons: the so-called KLEIN-GORDON equation. He attempted to transform SCHRÖDINGER's equation by making it invariant under any LORENTZ transformation; in 1928, he thus came up with his eponymous relativistic equation.

---

8. W. PAULI , « Physique moderne et philosophie », 1961, Ed. Albin Michel 1999, p. 108.

9. An inertial or Galilean frame of reference is a reference system (a marker) in which a body free from all interactions moves at a constant travelling speed.

This equation, which accounts for the odd half integer spin of electrons, predicted the existence of their antiparticles (positrons). These antiparticles would be discovered through experiments four years later by ANDERSON [10]. Therefore, we can safely say that special relativity is at the origin of the Standard Model (see section 4 of Point 3).

Special relativity has also had an impact on philosophy by eliminating any possibility of the existence of time and absolute duration anywhere in the Universe. In this context, the work of Henri POINCARÉ prompted philosophers, such as BERGSON, to ask different questions about time and space.

Einstein's theory of gravitation (general relativity) also fine-tunes KEPLER'S THEORY OF GRAVITY (see footnote 6, Point 3) by taking into account a wide range of phenomena including gravitational mirages [11].

In the same way, SCHRÖDINGER's quantum mechanics includes NEWTON's classic mechanics: by averaging the probability distribution of the presence of an electron (non-relativistic [12]) in an electromagnetic field, as obtained in quantum mechanics, we retrieve the results provided by Newtonian mechanics. Remember what MONTAIGNE said well before SCHRÖDINGER: "I can not fix my object; 'tis always tottering and reeling by a natural giddiness."

As far as elementary particles and their interactions are concerned and especially in terms of the 'construction and

---

10. C.D. ANDERSON, "The positive Electron," Physical Review, Vol. 43, 1933.
11. In a vacuum, light usually travels in a straight line; but in the Einsteinian space-time deformed by a massive celestial body (e.g. a cluster of galaxies), its trajectory is no longer straight as it follows the geodesics of this space. Therefore, a light source positioned behind such a cluster will appear to have one or more different positions from its actual angular position: this phenomenon is known as a gravitational mirage.
12. An electron whose speed is much slower than the speed of light in a vacuum.

dynamics' of life, quantum physics is perfectly satisfactory. The same applies to general relativity when large masses need to be taken into account. However, these two theories have not yet been unified, if indeed there is any reason to do so; at first glance, they seem irreconcilable. For example, time passes in a linear manner in quantum mechanics, whereas in general relativity it is a variable whose value depends on the presence of massive objects in the area where it is measured. String theory and loop quantum gravity, two approaches that aim more or less to achieve this objective have not yet been validated through experimentation. One major difficulty in this respect is that we do not know what happened during the 'Planck time' of our Big Bang i.e. 10^{-43} s.

Finally, it should be noted that there is not necessarily only one correct mathematical representation of the same physical phenomenon. Several distinct theoretical representations can correctly describe the same phenomenon. For example, in 1927 DIRAC demonstrated the equivalence between quantum mechanics in SCHRÖDINGER's representation (published in 1926) and HEISENBERG's representation (published in 1925).

3. Representations and the weight of their sense

Today, we know that our world is nothing like ARISTOTLE's for example. Using the images we have of our world to gain an understanding of its dynamics is at the heart of any scientific approach.

Matter, as our ancestors understood it, is not what it used to be. So, what is this fog of fermions interacting via bosons? We do not know! What is clear is that humans are dynamic lumps of unprecedented complexity. As ghosts in an elusive ontological reality, we seek, by trial and error, if not to grasp its substance then at least to understand its complex and far-reaching mechanisms.

Therefore, it is hardly surprising that many humans today are totally confused and disoriented. Yet peddlers of common sense, biding their time, still have a bright future ahead of them. And SPINOZA could still say almost four centuries on [13]:

> "Hence anyone who seeks for the true causes of miracles, and strives to understand natural phenomena as an intelligent being, and not to gaze at them like a fool, is set down and denounced as an impious heretic by those whom the masses adore as the interpreters of nature and the gods."

And writing of these practitioners of hermeneutics, these hucksters and purveyors of 'beliefs' elevated to the rank of intangible religious dogma, he added:

> "Such persons know that, with the removal of ignorance, the wonder which forms their only available means for proving and preserving their authority would vanish also."

The representations of the physics of the things of this world invite us to contemplate what we do not know and detect senses that do not ring true. They must be ceaselessly reviewed and improved as far as possible. Therefore, the

---

13. This quote by SPINOZA comes from the appendix to his first book on ethics.

evolution of these representations gives us a 'relative sense', which is constantly changing. The resulting philosophy could refine SCHOPENHAUER's philosophy of an absurd and meaningless world. In an attempt to understand what this relative sense might be, we will now make the distinction between 'living' on the surface of life and 'being' in its depths.

In our view, living on the surface of life like a bird in its treetop would be to feel and act in a continuous flow as part of our everyday representations of all things in our environment. We have our religious and political beliefs, our voluntary servitudes, our loves, our passions, etc. yet we confuse (often wrongly) the object-subjects concerned with the representations we have of them i.e. they seem to work or should work at our level.

On the other hand, being would involve contemplating the limitations of our representations and refining them where possible, thus improving the sense we have of Nature and Being; being would thus be the breath of a deeper breath of life.

Point 7

On the violence of life

Firstly, let us clarify what we mean by the violence of life from a physical point of view. This clarification will give us a better understanding of its full repercussions particularly with regard to the human condition and our societies.

As indicated in Point 3, the dynamics of Nature are analysed via four fundamental interactions i.e. gravitational, electromagnetic, and weak and strong nuclear interactions. Each of these interactions can cause very violent phenomena; for example, in gravity (see Point 4) the fusion of two neutron stars occurs via cataclysmic phenomena whose violence far exceeds the terrifying violence caused by the explosion of a *supernova*.

Lightning, fire, light, nanoscale physics, chemistry, molecular biology and indeed all life processes arise from electromagnetic interactions. Therefore, its mechanisms are, ultimately, a matter of quantum electrodynamics. Some electromagnetic phenomena are peaceful while others are extremely violent. For example, compare the soft light of a summer's evening to that produced in a lightning storm. This is true for all living things as the same interactions are involved.

1. Violence is consubstantial with life

In order to understand that the violence of all living organisms is inherent to life itself, we must evoke a principle concerning the evolution of the complexity of physical systems i.e. the second law of thermodynamics: the total entropy of an isolated system can never decrease over time.

In simple terms, this means that the complexity of such a system can only decrease. A system is considered to be isolated when it can not receive energy from external systems. For example, if we lived in a hermetically sealed room not eating, after a while we would cease to think eventually turning to dust and losing much of our original complexity. Nothing escapes this principle.

In common parlance, the concept of energy has several meanings. Here, we talk about energy as it is unambiguously defined in physics [1]. Similarly, the concept of power in physics has a well-defined meaning i.e. it is energy produced, transferred or consumed per unit of time. When discussing the essence of life, we will use the notion of power with this strict physical meaning. However, we may make a few exceptions e.g. the 'will to power' while remaining true to what has just been said.

At this point, we must point out that the process by which a system seeks its energy elsewhere in order to maintain or increase its complexity is relatively violent. For example, moving around using solar energy seems less violent to

---

1. In the International System of Units, energy is measured in Joules; an older unit is still sometimes used i.e. the calorie, which is equivalent to 4.18 Joules. Therefore, we might say that this meal has 800 kilocalories (Kcal).

us than burning fossil fuels. Similarly, we tend to forget the violence at the origin of the light that reaches us from our distant Sun just as we conveniently forget what happens in abattoirs as we enjoy a piece of meat.

Every living system fends of death for as long as it can by maintaining a precarious balance i.e. homoeostasis or its ability to maintain equilibrium in its environment regardless (or almost) of external constraints. Over the course of evolution and various geological times, homoeostasis has required ever more structures, complexity and superstructures; hence the need for ever more energy.

As we have seen, the concept of violence refers to the power consumed by a system for its survival but also to the original power it uses (of which it only uses a part) via its energy interfaces.

For us, violence also often takes on a special moral aspect. It is morally identified as such when this power is taken from others without their agreement. Moreover, if we do not provide a living system with the power it needs, we say that we are 'doing violence' [2] to it, especially if it is aware and suffers in consequence. In fact, we contribute to decreasing its complexity to the point of destroying it more or less quickly and violently.

Generally speaking, it is clear that violence is consubstantial with life. Let us delve deeper and turn our attention to plants and animals. Eukaryotes (etymologically those with a 'good nucleus': in ancient Greek 'eu' means 'good' and 'karyos' means 'nucleus') are living systems whose genetic

---

2. Scientists who have studied animal suffering found that lobsters and other crustaceans have complex nervous systems and feel pain when scalded. As a result of these findings, Swiss law now requires crustaceans to be stunned before they are killed.

material is stored inside the nucleus of their cells; incidentally, around 30% of the human gene pool is also found in cauliflowers. Therefore, here we will leave aside bacteria (which is not very considerate to them) which, via the chemical transformations they perform, are the slaves of eukaryotes. No doubt they also live off them and may occasionally use violence in return.

In general, plants are less violent than animals. The reason is simple: as they do not move about, the amount of power required for their survival and development is less than that required by animals, especially when the animal is large and heavy.

The transformations involved in the manufacture of plant cell proteins chiefly take place thanks to the minerals in the soil and the basic energy provided by light made possible by the quantum nature of the chlorophyll function (see section 1, Point 5).

Animals rely on more violent predation processes as nature documentaries like to show in graphic detail and whether vegetarian, carnivorous or omnivorous, they all feed on other eukaryotes i.e. they are all 'eukaryophagous'.

However, things are rarely simple and there are several species of carnivorous plants that can survive in nitrous-poor soils. We became omnivores via the ancestors of primates and fish.

Generally, the more complex a system becomes, the more we must expect violent actions in its external environment, at least in certain preliminary phases of its evolution. As a result, some animals, such as dolphins and humans, can be particularly violent and even cruel. Let us clarify this important point.

Any consciousness which perceives, even confusedly, some of the extraordinary potentialities of its vital momentum, may very well feel frustrated by the constraints of its environment i.e. the environment is perceived as hostile. In response, this consciousness, however partial, may engage in a process of anger. The power and resultant violence can prove devastating for its environment and itself. Sexual violence is a good example of this. The analysis of our psychological, sociological, economic and political behaviour could be enhanced by taking this elementary scientific and philosophical approach. For example, waving a flag to support our team at a sporting event is, very often, a form of 'primitive tribal euphoria' allowing us to forget for a while our more or less conscious frustrations.

Every human is an extremely complex biotype interacting with an even more complex environment. This biotope is the source of many more or less conscious acts of violence. For example, certain desires may conflict with one's idea of what is good or bad. Some individuals have even gone so far as to castrate themselves [3]. Generally, certain psychological conflicts can trigger processes of internal violence even affecting organs in the body such as the stomach or heart, as well as causing strokes in some cases. This is known as a psychosomatic reaction.

---

3. In Russia in the early 20th century, adepts of the Skoptzy sect still practised collective self-mutilation. They believed that Adam and Eve were guilty of having engaged in sexual intercourse and thus the only way to avoid sin was to perform self-castration.

2. Fear, ignorance and sacrificial violence

The first glimmering of consciousness among Homo sapiens was probably accompanied by a sense of wonderment and awe. No surprise there! What were they doing in this strange world full of plants, trees and animals? What did they think of the Sun, the days, the Moon and the myriad stars twinkling in the firmament? And what about the rain, wind, unleashed elements, lightning and fire?

They lived in a dog-eat-dog world and suffered all manner of injuries, as well as having to confront death: the death of their relatives, the death of women and babies in tragic childbirths, etc. In short, there was no time to think about their origins while all their energy was channelled into staying alive.

Facing violence from their peers and their environment, these hominids surely lived in almost constant fear and terror. Often they were forced to flee, take shelter in the natural world, hide in caves, lick their wounds, form clans, and start thinking about tools for hunting, revenge and war. To ensure their survival, their only option was to return this violence without limit and until death if necessary.

In addition to violence from their peers, whether close by or concealed, there were threats from animals and the heavens, although these were too far away to be understood. Therefore, they believed they must have angered the gods above, those sinister unknowns, who if not all-powerful were still the most powerful. To appease these gods, the primitive reflex was to offer them gifts in the form of victims. Thus began an era of sacrificial violence and scape-goating.

Sadly, a large part of humanity is still stuck in this age. Think about Shiite self-flagellation rites [4] and others forms of self-harm including those practised by Judeo-Christians [5].

Think of ABRAHAM who, channelling his fear and salvation (in the religious meaning of the word) into one god, was willing to sacrifice his only son; even today, some people are still willing to sacrifice that which they hold dearest. Besides, who has not done their best and, therefore, anything or almost anything to gain enlightenment? Yes, the depths of our ignorance regarding our raison d'être are bottomless.

3. A weighty legacy of violence

The following question is somewhat challenging: without the violence perpetrated by our ancestors, would we be able to perceive certain sublime harmonies of the world, such as those found in music, poetry, mathematics or even spirituality? The answer is no. We are bold living achievements in which biological and sociological predation mechanisms have played a decisive role over at least eight million years. Therefore, it is difficult to find a nation, civilisation or empire which existed without violence; there have always been wars, revolutions and other putschist periods followed by long

---

4. 'Tatbir' (in Arabic) is a self-flagellation ritual performed out of grief for the death of Mohammed's young grandson, Al-Husayn ibn Ali Talib, who was killed at the battle of Kerbala.

5. POPE JEAN-PAUL II was also familiar with the 'theology of sufferance'. He wore a cilice (or hair shirt) during lent and flagellated himself with his belt. At least this is what is stated in "Why he is a saint: the true JEAN-PAUL II", a book written in Italian by Bishop Slawomir ODER who was in charge of the beatification process of this former head of the Catholic church. These revelations show that this practice is still performed in this branch of Christianity. Yet suffering never saved anybody, on the contrary it just piles on more tragedy to the existing tragedy of life.

periods of stability, renunciation and oblivion. Once we realise this, a certain malaise sets in. Enjoying the sublime while forgetting where it really comes from seems to arise from a monstrous lack of consciousness; it would make us like those Schutzstaffel (SS) generals who, after 'visiting' a concentration camp, then went home and celebrated a cosy Christmas with their children. All things considered, the tragedy of living beings and the human story in particular, must be connected to this in some way. Thus we are not only cut off from god and the gods of yesteryear but also from what we as humans could become in a distant future. There is no reason why there should be a statute of limitations on this! Due to genetics and epigenetics, children are not free from the violence and crimes of their parents, it is simply agreed in law for the purposes of Living Together that they are innocent.

Therefore, we might come to the conclusion that in its evolution towards complexity and all that is akin to consciousness, life is an abomination of the laws of Nature, and by only retaining the best and forgetting all the crimes, some privileged people would say it is a miracle. We will let you be the judge of that; owing to certain fundamental biological inequalities, the answer can not be unanimous.

The Judeo-Christian concept of original sin is not as outdated as it would first appear as it reminds us of the very grave burden of being in this world. The Cathars thought that only a devil (Satan) had been able to weave the fabric of their being. But again things are rarely what they seem [6]. Christian BOBIN, a contemporary writer with a great interest in life and the living, says rather poetically: "I took the hand

---

6. C. BOBIN, « L'homme-joie », Ed. L'iconoclaste, 2012.

of the devil and saw light under his nails." In Point 8 we will discuss what kind of light he is talking about but first let us contemplate the shadows before making our way towards this light; a light that could dazzle and ultimately blind us.

4. The dominant, the dominated and hotbeds of violence

The principles, however democratic, which underpin the running of a multinational company, empire or even a country often plunge societies into spirals of wanton violence. On the grounds of satisfying the greatest number, or even provoking them, the aim is to constantly increase the sprawling complexity of the system to ensure that its power remains in the hands of a few egos or sometimes only one, the leader. This places the leader in a biologically dominant position rather like a queen bee in her hive. The whole system strengthens the leader's idea that it is Nature that gave him/her the power to rule. In his/her affairs, the leader is the dominant one or the one designated as such by Nature. The others, the implementers, the consumers, the ones left behind by evolution, in short Mother Nature's lost children, are the ones dominated by the system. Thus, from the top of the hill the proud stallion watches over his mares grazing in the safety of the valley below. Therefore, no matter the violence, humiliation and suffering caused by this frenetic accession to power, nor the epigenetic consequences affecting generations to come, and no matter the means put in place to safeguard it.

The CEO of a multinational corporation, a powerful empire, a country, a trade union or a political party, will not even see the effects of this violence. A whole system set up to protect the leader's dominant status and his/her entourage, will constantly remind the leader that acting in this way is for the common good i.e. you can't make an omelette without breaking eggs, etc. The leader will end up persuaded of this.

Yet this violence always leads to more violence perpetrated by the dominated. A violence that is often blind and devastating and which inevitably leads to the fall as it has in all empires from those of Charlemagne and Napoleon in Europe to the Han dynasty in China. The history of humanity is none other than an uninterrupted succession of dramatic events of this type.

In fact, everything indicates that the desire for power, possession and even posterity is based on a mimetic psychological structure; others inevitably reveal themselves as rivals who desire the same things as me. Thus desire concerns an object coveted by potential or real rivals; Eros carries within him the power of Thanatos, all the violence of death.

Violence and humiliation can also be brought about by cultural inequalities. The languages of knowledge are far from being accessible to all. Being able to understand the complex concepts of algebraic topology or the mathematics involved in general relativity or the Standard Model is not within everyone's intellectual reach. Therefore, the related languages and the knowledge they impart are reserved for a certain elite identified as such by those who might feel excluded. The most lucid among us understand that there are not only conceptual techniques in these fields; sometimes, there is beauty in Being. In many ways, these individuals can feel deeply frustrated and even humiliated. Wrongly, some will consider that what they hold most intimate and deepest, such as their self-respect, is undermined in this way. More often than not they will fall back on community, ethnic, political or religious reflexes, which may lead to disproportionate violence against those who have come to understand these languages and concepts. What has been illustrated by talking about mathematics also concerns spirituality and all the arts including music, sculpture, painting and poetry in particular. This can lead to a loss of self-confidence.

5. The violence of beliefs and principles

Among humans, clan systems are the source of much of the world's violence. Their raison d'être, development and power are founded on principles and ideas that can not easily be contested. Whether philosophical, religious, economic or political, these principles are always based on a questionable view of reality. Why? Quite simply because the dynamics of the world, and human psychology in particular, are not part of an equation that can be formulated or whose solution would be stable and robust even if it could.

To illustrate this point, let us first say a word about the obscurantism of revealed and institutionalised religions. The long list of related tragedies is lengthening throughout the world, particularly in the Middle East, Iran, Afghanistan, Pakistan, India, Sri Lanka and Indonesia. Those related to certain dogmatic Islamic discourses are well known in the West. Here, we will only discuss those linked to certain Christian beliefs. The extermination of the Cathers (see footnote 2, Point 6) already speaks volumes about what can be expected from obscurantism in general and its armed branches in particular. The two accounts presented below provide shocking examples.

The first concerns the tragic and horrific fate of HYPATIA of Alexandria. This remarkable woman of science and letters was both a philosopher and mathematician, as well as a prominent member of the Neoplatonic school in Alexandria where she taught philosophy and astronomy. This Greek woman was renowned in her own lifetime as a great teacher and a wise counsellor. In the fourth century C.E., she realised (among other things) that the Earth travels around the Sun in an elliptic orbit. She discovered this over a thousand years before KEPLER made the same discovery. For simply having grasped and clearly explained this phenomenon, she was stoned to death by a hoard of fanatical Christians.

The second tragic event concerns the fate of Giordano BRUNO who was burned alive in the Campo dei Fiori (the field of flowers) in Rome in February 1600 following an obscurantist verdict of the catholic church; a punishment still used in Islamic Sharia law [7].

Giordano BRUNO is one of many martyrs killed for daring to think freely. In this respect, it is important to point out that a Pontifical Commission by Pope JEAN-PAUL II, entitled "The Ptolemaic-Copernican controversy of the 16th and 17th centuries", instituted on 3 July 1981 revised its

---

7. In particular, this set of archaic and horrendous laws is enforced in the tiny state of Brunei. For example, since 3 April 2019, homosexuals and adulterous women can be punished by stoning.

conviction of GALILEO (by explaining the conjunctural circumstances) but reaffirmed the Church's formal conviction of Giordano BRUNO:

> Giordano BRUNO's conviction for heresy, regardless of one's views of the capital punishment he received *(everyone will understand the Church's evasion on this subject)*, appears to be entirely motivated on theological grounds as the Copernican heliocentrism of Giordano BRUNO is of no scientific interest.

Yet by showing that the movement of a body can not be considered in the absolute but only in relation to a reference system, Giordano BRUNO paved the way for the work of GALILEO. This principle based on the notion of an inertial frame of reference would also play a key role in the formulation of special relativity.

Now, let us consider societal violence brought about by certain principles such as the 'principle of equality'. It is important to note that this principle is supposed to underpin the legal and democratic functioning of our societies. In order to discuss this dispassionately, we should first clarify what is meant by 'equality' and 'law'. We know that from the very moment of conception every living being is genetically unique and irreplaceable. One individual's potential is not the same as another's; the process of conception is hence fundamentally unequal and we might even say fortunately so (or almost) as this is how life explores different avenues of possible development. This is why the 'transhumanist fantasy', which claims to be (in principle) egalitarian and fair is actually extremely worrying.

Love, like the desire to have a child with a certain partner, obeys the laws of biological symbiosis and these have nothing to do with equality. Diverse biological resonances prevail over any social understanding. Rightly or wrongly, the partners experiencing this love feel, via their five senses in particular, that their children (if conceived in this way) would enjoy an enriching natural equilibrium. By the same token, quantum biology tells us that the random conception of a human i.e. from partners who do not know each other well is similar to what could happen in a forced marriage or even rape; it denies the complexity of the living world and the deep quantum choices about its future. Therefore, it is irreversible genetic abuse of the unborn child. The right of the child should fall within limits based on the wisdom of reality.

As far as medically-assisted procreation is concerned, it is clear that total anonymity should be avoided. The donor and woman involved in this type of procreation should know each other at least virtually. It goes without saying that this would not prevent the donor from renouncing all rights concerning a child conceived in this manner.

That society tries to moderate, in terms of basic rights, the unequal effects of conception seems eminently desirable; this is what we are supposed to do in civilisations where humanity lingers on.

But what would happen in a society that, with the best of intentions, wanted to strictly apply the principle of equality? We already know the answer to this; its violence would ultimately come to resemble that which epitomises all totalitarian regimes past and present, such as North Korea.

Generally, the most devastating forms of violence are those that can truly be described as fundamentalist i.e. the violence which is unleashed when an individual, clan, sect, community, country or civilisation believes it holds the

'Truth' about the essence of things in this world. When the will to power fuels this insane fundamentalist fantasy nothing can stop its violence as it finds its justification in the assurance of being right.

Confronted with the sheer complexity of reality, humans who are a little more lucid show a certain humility as they are aware that their world representations and models, however sophisticated, have no ontological pretensions. They do not wish to alleviate the anguish of being in the world.

The positivism of the late nineteenth century has vanished and today's basic sciences are simply trying to identify representations that no longer make sense. Their spirituality of doubt, or perplexed spirituality, is often perceived as being negative. Then the practitioners of hermeneutics, those whom the masses adore in the words of SPINOZA, return to the fray. But as always, they can only provide nonsensical answers to poorly posed questions. This is how fundamentalism sinks its teeth into naive people who have never been trained in critical thinking. Sheltering behind the shield of their convictions, they will happily slit the throat of the unbeliever or the *kâfir* (as they are called in Arabic in Islam). This is how all types of ideological, religious and political convictions first unleash and exacerbate the existential violence of our reptilian and limbic brains; the neocortex gives them the right to act violently with no holds barred.

6. A glimmer of hope

The harmonies of the good and beautiful are also a part of the potential of quantum electrodynamics, although it is the hostile achievements that seem to prevail in the majority of cases. Everything indicates that the probability of hostile achievements happening outweighs the good ones.

However, in terms of demographics and political economy, the idea of unrestricted growth is already beginning to falter. This insane growth is almost desperate as it occurs on contradictory bases: an unbridled desire for consumption and the fear of war. Our planet has limited resources and if we continue as we are, we must expect a dramatic finale. We can only hope for a positive reaction from the system before it is too late.

Our societies are still a long way off from assimilating the twentieth century's scientific advances in basic research. In fact, these advances are still only interested in the resultant technical and industrial applications. Yet these applications often distance us from our poetic inclinations and spiritual potential for creativity. Through sharing and dialogue, we can be hopeful about a positive exit from the current situation.

Everything that is amiss in this world prompts us to direct our gaze towards what can enlighten it, namely what we have called in the following Point: Nature's harmonies. The question then arises of knowing how to free ourselves from the violence of life to access the harmonies of Being, which in Nature are often veiled or even hidden.

In our increasingly rudderless societies, science can provide some responses. The appearance of life and its evolution shows us that the impulse towards good and its related virtues owes more to harmonious alliances than to conflicting rivalries, even if chivalrous. And so it is the case in our own biosphere and on all scales, from nanoscale interactions in biochemistry to cultural and civilisational interactions in humanity.

Taking a slightly optimistic view of the future of humankind, we may wish for a gradual *metanoia*: a reversal by which humanity would open up to something greater than itself. It is hoped that in the medium term, education, the media and social networks will guide humans towards more acceptable representations of their presence in the world.

 **Point 8**

Nature's harmonies

In Nature some phenomena are clearly harmonious while others are less so and how they are perceived depends on the living organism in question. For example, what was harmonious to MOZART might not be for a migrating bird but in both cases it is a question of resonance. A certain cerebral sensitivity resonates with a natural phenomenon thus the harmonic structures of music for MOZART and the distribution of the Earth's magnetic field for a migrating bird.

Highlighting the founding nature of pre-Socratic approaches, it is important to bear in mind that it was undoubtedly PYTHAGORAS and his followers who first became aware of the harmonies of music and number theory. According to ARISTOTLE [1], these philosophers realised that all forms of musical harmony and their underlying relationships were governed by proportional numbers.

1. Harmonies and their possible sense

One major aim of humankind is to identify harmonies that could have sense. In one of his books [2] KUNDERA, despairing the finiteness of representations of things thus

---

1. ARISTOTLE, *Metaphysics*, A, 5, p. 57.
2. M. KUNDERA, "The Festival of Insignificance", Ed. Gallimard, 2013.

champions insignificance. However, he is not referring to 'insignificance' in the strict meaning of the word. In fact quite the opposite, in a kind of poetic meditation he seeks to perceive Nature's hidden harmonies; in this case, a choir of children arranged in a perfect semi-circle preparing to sing the French national anthem in the Luxembourg Gardens in Paris. Yet before they begin, the sleigh of Stalin, who wanted to impose his representation of the world through his own will, must first leave the Gardens. The Festival of Insignificance is therefore a novel about exploring hidden harmonies.

The contemporary poet Christian BOBIN (quoted earlier) entitled one of his books 'La Grande Vie'[3] implying that there are lives in which the harmonies of Being are veiled:

> "What is lacking in this world is not money or even what we call sense or meaning but rather the river of children's eyes, and the cheerfulness of squirrels and angels."

It is to this life that we will turn our gaze; this indescribable life. As we have already seen, this life emerges from the awesome potentialities of quantum electrodynamics. Neuronal man is just a highly simplified version of the hyper-complex quantum ecosystems of his being. Nobody can claim to truly understand these ecosystems and so we must be satisfied with having an idea or notion of them. As Jean FERRAT sang in a poem by ARAGON: "The poet is always right", so let us hear from Christian BOBIN once again: "I took the hand of the devil and saw light under his nails."

The beauty of mathematics, representations of theoretical physics and all cultural, artistic and poetic creations

---

3. C. BOBIN, « La grande vie », Ed. Gallimard, 2014.

mysteriously emerge on the surface of life via fabulous and indescribable quantum architectures. Naturally, the likelihood of these concepts and virtues arising is low if not non-existent. The same is true for the deep bonds of fraternity and love in the sense of *agapê*.

Think how surprised or even exhilarated we can sometimes feel when we perceive beauty or divine music; it as almost as if they came to us from another world. Spiritualist thinkers – like BERGSON and JANKÉLÉVITCH – said they arose from Nature's vital momentum.

Among the genetic mutations that made the emergence of life possible, those that enabled it to continue and become more complex gradually imposed themselves while those that did not died out. This is how the vital momentum eventually found its way into the genome of the living world as we see it today. Having said that, scientists in the twentieth century were already aware of the incredible complexity of the physical phenomena involved in this structuring of living things. Based on the fundamental contributions of DIRAC and FEYNMAN, we now understand that this vital momentum is registered in the genome via the prodigious potentialities of quantum electrodynamics. Today, this is widely accepted, at least insofar as everything related to the body's biological infrastructure so its cells, neurons, neurotransmitters, hormones, etc.

While the definition of the human body is generally agreed upon, it is not always the case with the concepts of the 'soul' or 'mind'. As far as the soul is concerned, the definition we have implicitly adopted up to now is to associate it with the complex system of the unconscious and the conscious emotions of the neuronal body. Thus the mind would be related to all manner of hyper-complex thought dynamics that would occasionally allow us to glimpse the subtle beauties of Being (as defined in the foreword of this essay). This mind, not to be confused with the related intellect, which arises from the neural approximation of the thinking body would be a kind of 'bioluminescence of the soul', which is no small matter for us. However, without the body's infrastructures which are not always very attractive [4], there would be no soul nor any possibility of mind perception.

Scientists now agree that life systems are all the more unpredictable because they are complex. Therefore, there is no longer any fundamental opposition between spirituality and matter provided we take matter to mean the potential offered by the interaction of fermions via photons. By this we mean that current representations of matter are a long way away from the atomism of DEMOCRITUS.

2. Is the living world beautiful?

Continuing with our exploration, let us consider what a spiritualist with one foot in the West and one in the East, such as François CHENG, thinks of our world. In one of his books [5] he says:

> "Along the paths of existence, we come up against two fundamental mysteries, the mystery of beauty and the

---

4. This is one of the reasons why the Cathars were unable to accept the idea of the 'incarnation of Christ'; they believed that Jesus had to have a tangible body only in appearence. Facing an inquisition hearing today, a lawyer could use the argument that the bodies of the living i.e. the tunics of the poor Cathars like that of Christ are of a very low density (compared to that of neutron stars for example). Photons sweep through space far more frequently than fermions.

5. F. CHENG, « Cinq Méditations sur la mort. Autrement dit sur la vie », Ed. Albin Michel, 2013.

mystery of evil. Beauty is mysterious because the universe was not obliged to be beautiful. Whereas it happens that it is, and that seems to reveal a desire, an appeal, a hidden intentionality that can leave no one indifferent."

He goes even further: "It would be in bad faith not to admit that the living universe is beautiful."

Most of us would readily agree that the living world is beautiful but only if we retain what seems beautiful to us. In other words, we could say that François CHENG has donned a pair of rose-coloured spectacles and he is surely not alone in this! Many documentary makers are awed by this 'universal beauty' yet when they talk about stunning natural ecosystems (which we must try to protect), they find it difficult to hide the exorbitant cost of this beauty i.e. the violence that is consubstantial with all life [6]. In the Old Testament, ISAIAH (chapter 11, verse 6) can only resolve the problem by dreaming of a better world in the future:

> The wolf shall dwell with the lamb, and the leopard shall lie down with the young goat, and the calf and the lion and the fattened calf together; and a little child shall lead them.

Children's stories often try to hide this violence. We condition them – from infancy – not to see the reality. They will have plenty of time for that later. And besides, who has never donned a pair of rose-coloured spectacles themselves?

---

6. In a documentary about the EUROPA ISLAND NATIONAL RESERVE, Nicolas HULOT is forced to agree. Towards the end of his documentary about this unique ecosystem, Nicolas Hulot tries to save recently hatched green turtles by transporting them from their nests to the beach. However, the voracity of the predatory birds and patrolling frigates defeats his attempts; we can hear the sadness in his voice.

The world of plants often seems more beautiful than that of animals and it is certainly less violent. This is normal as the quantum universe of plants is less ambitious than that of animals. In fact, the mere fact that the comparative form is used here says more about this point then any argument. That said, from the brightly-coloured fish in the coral reefs to the rats in our sewers, what worries us most are their eyes; they convey to us, without knowing why, the absolute necessity to maintain their respective homoeostasis. Is all this beautiful? It is up to each of us to think and react in our own way. We believe that Being could have done a better job in terms of its potential achievements.

Most people would generally agree that a deer is more pleasing to the eye than a wild boar. Some might even say that a fine horse is more beautiful than a handsome man so much so that we ended up clothing the latter and not just to offer protection from the elements! Man has been 'civilised' in so many ways that he has become a 'superior' being almost liberated from his animal condition. In summer, the majority of socialised humans would instinctively turn their gaze from a nudist beach. Seeing man in all his nakedness perturbs the soul.

Now, let us turn our attention towards the entrails of living organisms. Take the example of a lion devouring a gazelle: for us this is horrific! Millions of years of evolution and suffering to get to this! No! Let us zoom in. On a millimetric scale, it is already more acceptable and at the nanometric scale it is practically sublime: a beautiful quantum architecture simply falling apart at its own pace. The elegant beauty of a gazelle appeals us to more than a rat. Yet on the nanoscale i.e. in the realm of fermions and photons, couldn't there be a universal beauty in all living things?

The majority of scientists have the following reaction. Certain quantum electrodynamics achievements are magnificent while most others are less so. For example, the various molecules involved in making lavender perfume are prodigious while the molecules associated with foul odours (e.g. rotten eggs), namely hydrogen sulphide (H_2S), are far less so.

Yet when it come to the dynamics of life, what should we think? Beautiful or not? Under certain conditions, a methyl CH_3 radical will bind to a piece of DNA in a beautiful way by activating the positive potential of the genome (see section 3, Point 5). In other situations this same radical will, by binding itself elsewhere, eliminate certain immune defences or even block certain evolutionary potentialities.

Generally, we perceive some chemical reactions as being beautiful (and good) and others as ugly (and evil). Hence, using the same chemical ingredients you could either make a fabulous firework or cause a terrible explosion. In brief, beauty and good, like ugliness and evil, are all products of quantum electrodynamics. However, these achievements are not binary; the products of the living do not fall into two categories of beautiful (and good) and ugly (and evil).

3. Is there a hidden intentionality?

Now let us consider the hidden intentionality discussed by François CHENG; a point of view also shared by Jean d'ORMESSON. In one of his books [7], one chapter is entitled

---

7. J. d'ORMESSON, « Je dirai malgré tout que cette vie fut belle », Gallimard, 2016.

"Above us there is something like an unknown power". The use of "like" is extremely perceptive; Jean d'ORMESSON thus defends himself from any accusations of anthropomorphism. Otherwise, the premise would be that creation was the work of an external intelligent entity. That said, his assertion may lend credence to the idea that Nature is a powerful random achievement of Being (see the foreword of this essay).

For most physicists, Nature is an ontologically inaccessible substance as its manifestations are in perpetual metamorphosis. The fact that in the chaotic transition phase of our Big Bang, it adopted certain simple and stable mathematical structures (notably those of quantum electrodynamics, which made life possible) does not mean it is a perfectly successful achievement of the potentialities of Being (see footnote 5, Point 3). In fact, everything seems to indicate that its event-driven dynamics were random and hazardous, and were certainly not characterised by the careful deployment of resources making it not very ecologically-friendly either!

In brief, its rare success tend to make us overlook its very many failures. TEILHARD de CHARDIN always tried to reconcile the irreconcilable and even said [8]: "Creating is no small affair for the Almighty, a pleasure. It's an adventure, a risk and a battle He is fully involved in."

---

8. M. SCHMITZ, « Teilhard de Chardin », Ed. EDILIVRE-APARIS, 2014.

4. Promoting harmonious alliances

For beauty and good to occur and prosper and even prevail, subtle conditions of partnership and exchange, which are difficult to establish and maintain in practice, must be in place. As for hope, we must give time more time.

Societies that develop on the basis of unhealthy alliances are short-lived for the same reasons that certain overly fragile chemical structures only last for a very short time as their structural alliances and chemical bonds are fundamentally unstable. For example, we can conjecture that before the emergence of bacteria and eukaryotes, other life forms tried to come into being but did not succeed for these reasons.

Similarly, societies promoting unbridled liberalism are heading toward their demise. Theocratic, religious and/or totalitarian regimes founded on intangible dogmas, are also condemned in the medium term without appeal.

Establishing harmonious alliances means identifying in each of us (in each community, culture and civilisation) what is best in order to bring out even more prodigious achievements thanks to the alchemy of the exchange and sharing; to retain what the vital momentum (in the meaning outlined above) has done best so far in the diversity of souls, and the plurality of spiritualities, arts and sciences. If we believe we are able to judge the more or less harmonious nature of these achievements, then there must be a related hierarchy. And even if there is disagreement as to the order of this hierarchy, it does seem to exist in the potentialities of Being beyond any subjectivity. As mentioned in Point 6, it is out of the question to consider in a politically correct relativistic [9] manner, that everything is or would be worthwhile. In other words, we may be wrong in our appreciation of what is harmonious and what is not, nevertheless we believe this hierarchy exists.

Instead of trying to better each other in stupid competitions, or stun each other with various behaviours and absurd violence, our cultural history should encourage us to think and collaborate together. However, it takes time for harmonious links to be woven and permeate the memory of the living. In the meantime we must protect ourselves in the long term from the untimely violence of certain catastrophic achievements of the living, such as those perpetrated in totalitarian regimes (religious or otherwise). By acting in this way in all areas with perplexity, vigilance and wisdom, our existential adventure could continue towards a brighter, or at least a less dark, future. However, it will still be necessary to ensure that our biosphere is not overly affected by the external natural phenomena that also condition our survival within it.

---

9. That is to say, it is related to the philosophy of 'relativism', a movement of thought that has nothing to do with relativity in physics.

■ Point 9

Beliefs and spirituality

An often very poorly posed question is: do you believe in god? What does 'god' actually mean to the person asking the question? It is important to know the answer to this before a response can be given. As for the question of believing not only does it implicitly raise further questions about the nature of this god but also about what we understand by existence. Each time we try to represent something as it exists, we almost always realise (after fine-tuning our observations) that what we end up with does not correspond to our initial idea. This is true for the atom which, etymologically, means 'not able to be cut'. Yet atoms can be divided as they are made up of various subatomic particles i.e. electrons and quarks interacting via bosons. However, in this world, the question of 'separability' is no longer posed in classical terms (see footnote 4 of Point 2, and section 1 of Point 3).

In order to shed light on the discussion of what 'god' means, we will consider firstly a god who is a 'creator' in the transcended image of man, and secondly another who is a 'great watchmaker' devising the harmonies of Nature.

If God were simply the Principle of Being i.e. 'what' makes being Being without any causality, it would be very hard not to believe since Being is a fact and we would not be here talking about it if it were not. It goes without saying that 'what' Being is does not have to be an entity with recognisable or observable intent. This type of god is probably the closest to the god described by SPINOZA (*"Deus sive Natura"*, God i.e. Nature).

1. A creator in the transcendent image of mankind

Others, who believe in a more interventionist god i.e. one with a clearly identifiable will of his own (e.g. like the god of the Talmud, Bible or Koran), would soon stop believing in him once they had taken note of certain irrefutable facts concerning, in particular, the position of the Earth in the Universe, the evolution of the tree of life throughout the various geological ages, the catastrophic events which dramatically changed the position of hominids on this tree, etc. It is a good thing that in today's civilisations, some people have been able to shrug off the beliefs of yesteryear; fortunately, spirituality is not limited to naive credulity.

The god of the Old Testament is clearly a 'transcended patriarchal image' of man. And as VOLTAIRE neatly put it: "If God has made us in his image, we have returned the favour."

In many ways, the New Testament is revolutionary compared to the Old Testament. One could even say that Jesus demystified our access to spirituality. In its cultural and religious context, this spirituality was reserved for the practitioners of hermeneutics of the time i.e. the high priests of the ancient Jewish religion. And as for many of those who try to make the world a better place, Jesus paid the highest price!

Yet what should we think, for example, about the parable of the 'birds of the sky'? According to the gospel of Saint Matthew (chapter 6, verse 26), Jesus implored his disciples not to hoard:

> Look at the birds of the air; they do not sow or reap or store away in barns, and yet your heavenly Father feeds them. Are you not much more valuable than they?

By urging us not to worry about the future, these words of wisdom encourage us to live on the surface of life like the birds in their trees. The profound aspiration of Christian BOBIN on "the cheerfulness of squirrels and angels" also originates this from this hesitant soul-searching (or mind searching). It is wonderfully poetic and socially informative but what is it really about? We all know how fearful birds are and how they must battle to stay alive. Like their distant theropod ancestors, they can not escape the violence that is consubstantial with all life. And anyway, what makes humans more 'valuable' than birds? In fact, Jesus was implicitly referring here to the second commandment in verse 28 (chapter one) of the Book of Genesis:

> Rule over the fish in the sea and the birds in the sky and over every living creature that moves on the ground.

Given that the representations in the Book of Genesis in the Torah were of this order, how then could Jesus have seen living things as we see them today?

And what exactly is 'salvation'? It is certainly a question much debated in Christian communities. Is it a way of rescuing Christians from evil so they can enjoy a state of eternal happiness in a new world? This is what Jesus and his apostles preached: accept the gospel and receive salvation, refuse and perish! But what is this evil we must be saved from? And what about animals? Evil and violence had been around for millions of years long before the painful emergence of homo sapiens! But naturally Jesus did not know this. For today's Christians, does this mean grafting some type of profound sense onto our poor animal condition? In many ways, this potentially dangerous heavenly dream has turned out to be just that (see section 5, Point 7). Yet in the context of a time when adulterous women were stoned to death, Jesus (like the apostle Paul) could only approach these questions as an idealistic humanist. In fact it was high time to start putting oneself in the place of others, naturally with all the risks of error related to such an attitude if one were to abuse it...

Obviously, the existence of this god naturally goes beyond all the evils associated with institutionalised religions. Let us read what DIRAC had to say about this at the Solvay Conference of 1927:

"I don't know why we are talking about religion. If we are honest – and scientists have to be – we must admit that religion is a jumble of false assertions with no basis in reality. The very idea of God is a product of the human imagination. It is quite understandable why primitive people, who were so much more exposed to the overpowering forces of nature than we are today, should have personified these forces in fear and trembling. But nowadays, when we understand so many natural processes, we have no need for such solutions. I can't for the life of me see how the postulate of an Almighty God helps us in any way. What I do see is that this assumption leads to such unproductive questions as why God allows so much misery and injustice, the exploitation of the poor by the rich and all the other horrors He might have prevented. If religion is still being taught, it is by no means because its ideas still convince us, but simply because some of us want to keep the lower classes quiet. Quiet people are much easier to govern than clamorous and dissatisfied ones. They are also much easier to exploit. Religion is a kind of opium that allows a nation to lull itself into wishful dreams and so forget the injustices that are being perpetrated against the people. Hence the close alliance between those two great political forces, the State and the Church. Both need the illusion that a kindly God rewards – in heaven if not on earth – all those who have not risen up against injustice, who have done their duty quietly and uncomplainingly. That is precisely why the honest assertion that God is a mere product of the human imagination is branded as the worst of all mortal sins."

These ideas of DIRAC remind us of the major considerations common to Marxists, *Proudhonistes*, communists and traditional anarchists: the opium of the people, neither God nor Master, etc. It invites us to challenge the peddlers of humbug who persist in talking to us about god; hence the very relevant analysis of the exploitation of credulity in order to alienate the weak from the strong [1].

But this means forgetting, rather quickly, that there are natural dispositions towards spirituality within the structures of the mind. According to the latest neuroscience research,

---

1. In 1927, while DIRAC was concerned about the relationship between the State and Church, negotiations between Pope Pius XI and Mussolini, which resulted in the Lateran Treaty in February 1929, had been underway for around a year. Under the terms of this concordat Catholicism is recognised as the sole religion of the Italian State thus making Catholic religious education compulsory at all school levels..

the dispositions of our mental universe are the result of the evolution of homo sapiens over at least 300,000 years. Humans, who gradually become aware of the violence of life and their environment, created 'spiritual systems' in their brains and in women in particular owing to the care they had to give to children. Based on this simple observation, we could speculate that on average women are more disposed to spirituality than men. These systems are often passed on to their DNA through subtle epigenetic mechanisms. These humans would have less trouble surviving thus explaining why, even today, some individuals are better equipped than others.

In the 1980s, by stimulating the temporal lobes of the brains of around one hundred people with weak electromagnetic fields, Michael PERSINGER [2] managed to induce mystical feelings and the awareness of a universal truth associated with elation in around 80% of his subjects. Naturally, these feelings varied depending on the culture and religion of the subjects. They spoke of god or the Buddha, and feelings of total oneness with the Universe as well as an incredible sense of euphoria. PERSINGER came to believe that it was very probable that the most exalted figures in the major religions (Mohammed, the Buddha, Moses, Paul on the road to Damascus, etc.) may have suffered from a form of epilepsy occurring in the temporal lobe.

Similarly, in a study published in 2001, Andrew NEWBERG [3] demonstrated that when Tibetan monks

---

2. His experiments ended in scientific controversy; see St-PIERRE LS, PERSINGER MA, "Experimental facilitation of the sensed presence is predicted by the specific patterns of the applied magnetic fields, not by suggestibility: re-analyses of 19 experiments," International Journal of Neuroscience 116 (9): 1079-96, 2006.

(participating in the study) reached the peak of their meditative trance, their brains showed increased activity in the right pre-frontal lobe coupled with decreased activity in the parietal lobe. This frontal lobe is mainly involved in planning and attention. The increase in its activity could reflect the practice in Buddhist meditation of focusing intensely on a thought or object. One of the chief functions of the parietal lobe is to situate and evolve an individual in space. The profound and abnormal silence experienced during meditation would support the feelings reported by these monks of "letting go of the ego" and "oneness with the Universe". Finally, the increase in activity observed in the limbic system, which is strongly linked to emotions, adds to the feeling of well-being associated with this sensation of cosmic oneness.

In 2006, NEWBERG [4] conducted further experiments on religious practices finding that some people start speaking in gibberish or languages (known as glossolalia) that can only be understood by god and the angels. Glossolalia is linked to certain religious and spiritual cults especially charismatic Christian ones, such as the Pentecostals, who see it as a manifestation of the 'Holy Spirit' and refer to this 'gift' as 'speaking in tongues'. In the modified states of consciousness of the five people who participated in the study, NEWBERG observed a decrease in activity in the frontal lobes. This could explain the loss of control necessary for the spectacular expression of mystical fervour occurring during glossolalia.

3. NEWBERG AB, ALAVI A, Baime M, POURDEHNAd M, SANTANNA J, d'AQUILI EG. Newberg AB, Alavi A, Baime M, Pourdehnad M, Santanna J, d'Aquili EG, "The measurement of regional cerebral blood flow during the complex cognitive task of meditation: A preliminary SPECT study," Psychiatry Research: Neuroimaging 106: 113-122, 2001.
4. NEWBERG AB, "Tongues on the Mind," Science, November 10, 2006.

More critical conditions also provide us with information about the brain's potential for elation. For example, an American neurobiologist recounted how, after suffering a brain haemorrhage, her soul and spirit seemed to float free. Her usual perception of the constraints related to her presence in the world completely vanished. She found herself in a spiritual and pleasurable state of consciousness. Everything returned to normal following treatment for the haemorrhage.

The important thing to take away from this neuroscience research and related observations is that the various forms of well-being, ecstasy and elation developed through mystical practices must surely challenge the beliefs of followers of the religions in question. The temptation to have faith in their beliefs is naturally very strong but what about the legitimacy of the dogmatic expressions of their spirituality? Wouldn't this mean that fabulous stories could only originate from the doctrinal imagination of those who founded and structured their religions?

The result of all these ideas can be summed up very neatly in the popular adage 'don't throw the baby out with the bath water'. In this case, the baby represents spirituality (*agapê*, poetry, music and the arts in general) while the bathwater represents the violence of unfounded representations put forward by those who talk about spirituality and even awaken it sometimes.

The musical and architectural achievements of religious art, regardless of the trials and tribulations that motivated them, say far more than a protracted debate on the subject. These spiritual dispositions are the birthplace of all the arts, gifts and talents worthy of these names. To say that this spirituality is not rooted in the animality of our human condition would be to objectively deny who we really are in terms of Nature. However, we still have the right to think that 'the scent of this spirituality' can sometimes allow us to glimpse, albeit very rarely, certain fabulous potentialities of Being.

Churches, temples, synagogues and mosques could gradually become places of reflection, contemplation and culture where people could gather to meditate and nurture their spirituality. We could finally renounce, without sadness or regret, the hope of finding a deeper sense therein; only its beneficent, gentle and peaceful shadow would remain.

2. A great watchmaker devising nature's harmonies

Later in his life, Dirac's ideas about god were tempered. In May 1963, in an article in Scientific America, he wrote:

> "It seems to be one of the fundamental features of nature that fundamental physical laws are described in terms of a mathematical theory of great beauty and power, needing quite a high standard of mathematics for one to understand it. You may wonder: Why is nature constructed along these lines? One can only answer that our present knowledge seems to show that nature is so constructed. We simply have to accept it. One could perhaps describe the situation by saying that God is a mathematician of a very high order, and He used very advanced mathematics in constructing the universe. Our feeble attempts at mathematics enable us to understand a bit of the universe, and as we proceed to develop higher and higher mathematics we can hope to understand the universe better."

These words of DIRAC are very different from what we read earlier being far more humble and uncertain and thus wiser, as well as echoing VOLTAIRE's anthropomorphic statement: "There can be no watch without a watchmaker." It also reflects the views of the spiritualist thinkers discussed in Point 8. The violence of life could be to the harmonies of the world what the dominant seventh chord is to the perfect chord; the dissonances of the former are resolved in the harmonic frequencies of the latter: its fundamental frequency and its three multiples. Here we find the Omega point of TEILHARD de CHARDIN: his "Cosmic Christ".

We tend to think that Nature i.e. that which arose amid the chaos of our Big Bang is only one achievement among many others of the potentialities of Being; thus we can conjecture that its mathematical structures are not as complex as those of Being. For a neo-Cathar, Satan (the creator of the world) would be a very poor mathematician indeed.

◤ Point 10

Acting in a fraternity of the incomplete

First, let us explain what we mean here by 'fraternity'. As explained in Points 1 and 2, it is clear that sense emerges from the complexity of life. This is especially true of fraternity in its deepest and most intimate aspects. Let us try to flesh out this very subtle aspect of life.

According to Spinoza: "We believe we are free because we are unaware of the causes which determine us"; we are free to feel empathy or aversion to someone. Bohr, a pioneer of quantum physics, would probably say now: we believe we are free because we are unaware of the 'fuzzy causes' that determine us. Indeed, this is what seems to result from experiments which confirm the principle of superposition of possible quantum physical states. As we saw in Point 5, this principle allows us to better understand the profound texture of life.

To put it plainly, Bohr would be right while Spinoza would have an overly deterministic view of the things of this world. Einstein would have thought the same; remember what he said at the Solvay Conference in 1927: "God doesn't play with dice". In any case, the main thing is to seek, as far as possible, those causes that determine us especially in terms of our empathy for certain people, although this would not be easy for at least two reasons.

First of all, we do not know which equations would make it possible to model the behaviour of a biological system even one as elementary as that of a single living cell, be it plant or animal. And even if we could, we already know from experience that the solutions to this equation would be very sensitive to the constraints imposed on this dynamic system.

Therefore, it is impossible, *a priori*, to truly reflect on the reason of affects and the affect of reason. If we could, we this would then be at the very heart of the intimacy of the affect of fraternity and the strength of its reason! Therefore, it is not surprising that in the concept of Living Together, fraternity has a fluid unspecified sense. On our scale, we can undoubtedly perceive a fuzzy link of a warm essence whose mystery must be preserved.

1. Solidarity and fraternity

Thinking about fraternity leads us to consider our way of being of society. For example, philosophers like Bruno Mattéi have long understood that fraternity is not the same as solidarity [1].

Etymologically speaking, solidarity refers to the notion of 'solidity'; the interactions that bind certain entities together in a relatively rigid manner. For example, in a diamond each carbon atom is linked to four others. None of its electrons are free and it is does not conduct heat very well making it beautiful yet cold. In terms of humans, we could say that solidarity maintains the cohesion of a social group

---

1. B. MATTÉI, « Envisager la fraternité », Revue Projet (n° 330), 2012/5, pages 66-74.

but in a rather cold way. These diverse 'solidarity interactions' are frequent albeit somewhat tepid.

Other less frequent interactions resonate with us or reveal, more intimately, the potentialities of the parties brought together in this way. For example, the aromatic character of a benzene molecule results from its quantum wave nature in which its six atoms of carbon and hydrogen share six electrons (see section 1, Point 3). In a diagram of this molecule, we represent this sharing by a small circle placed in the middle of the hexagonal structure. This reminds us (for example) the 'circularity' of the *agapê* in the Last Supper painted by Leonardo de VINCI.

In quantum physics, there can be no resonance without interaction. However, an interaction which ensures the cohesion of an ensemble does not necessarily mean that its elements are resonating to the point where they are participating in a 'warmly scented' dance. Therefore, it is not surprising that in humans in particular, solidarity does not necessarily imply a fraternity worthy of the name or indeed an associated warm action; but fraternity does imply associated links of solidarity .

It is important to differentiate between the fraternity which is at the heart of any life system i.e. the intra-fraternity and inter-fraternity that expresses the crossed potentialities of these systems.

2. Intra-fraternity

Let us start with the warm fraternity that animates all 'dynamic life systems'. This intra-fraternity defines a local good, an ecological niche or a family (in the broadest meaning) that contributes to the survival, development and fulfilment of the elements of this system within, of course, its 'interactional limitations'.

To clarify this point, let us consider the religious fraternity (in the etymological meaning of the term) of the ecumenical monastic community of Taizé in Burgundy. Its interactional limitations result from its members' world view, a view that does not, in many respects, correspond to what humans are in Nature.

To support this point, let us look at the circumstances surrounding the murder of this community's founder, Brother Roger, who was stabbed to death on 16 August 2005 during evening prayers. The murderer, a Romanian woman called *Luminata Solcanu* suffered from severe psychiatric problems and had been removed from the community on the grounds that she was unstable. In the world view of this community, men and women have a conscience and a clear free will to love, without limit, a single, good and perfect God, the creator of this world. This belief essentially underpins this community. Therefore, if one of its members does not fit their standard definition of a human, does this mean that evil and therefore Satan was somehow involved? It is clear that humans, who interact with the billions of bacteria that inhabit them, are not so simple. It may be that an individual seeking the absolute in a part of his/her brain where sublime 'quantum fraternities' reign is in total imbalance in another part. Perhaps because in this part of their brain certain proteins are missing and hence other fraternities too. In this case, it is the latter that (along with many others) contribute to the emergence of a more or less clear conscience.

The aforementioned community questioned this violent death in a publication entitled "La mort de frère Roger, pourquoi ?" [NB: The death of Brother Roger, why?] [2]. The answer was clear: "Brother Roger was an innocent, a man for whom things were self-evident and which had an immediacy not as readily apparent to others". This community provided an interpretation of his murder which, instead of questioning its founding principles, was 'instinctively' used to 'sanctify' their value even further as is so often the case! 'Clan fraternities' do their best and can sometimes be useful but unfortunately they are, to say the least, closed while naturally claiming they are not.

What precisely defines a clan group is that it excludes anything or anybody that could undermine its founding principles. Thus clan fraternities harbour often unbeknownst to themselves the seeds of their own downfall. This is also how biological brothers can end up killing each other. For example, the horrific ongoing conflict tearing apart the Palestinian Arab and Hebrew communities is well-known but it is essentially because their genomes (in the broadest meaning) are so close! A very long-term aim would not be to create two states in Palestine living peacefully side by side but rather to create one.

More generally, let us consider the case where the potentialities of a dynamic life system can not fraternise with those of another nearby. What would happen is that the two systems would ignore each other or if encounters were unavoidable they might engage in conflict resulting in the potential destruction of one or both, as well as wiping out their local harmonies. In the event of such an encounter, the life

---

2. Internet source: https://www.taize.fr/fr_article3786.html.

process fails. The entropy of the two systems increases: the good associated with their order is dissolved locally into the evil of their respective death disorder. If it is not careful, humanity might also disappear in the medium term. However, life perseveres relentlessly until it thrives i.e. until there are inter-fraternal potentialities which encounters can reveal and harmoniously exploit. Let us thus follow a 'positive path' towards inter-fraternity.

3. Inter-fraternity

In humans, especially at the civilisational level, strong inter-fraternity potentialities can be masked by glaring incompatibilities linked to very different conceptual representations of the things of this world. We can see that, based on the local fraternities which underpin our current societies, we must urgently move towards a far more fraternal and humanist globalisation but we still have a long way to go despite the fact that our very existence as a species is at risk!

Life and earth sciences talk about the unconscious fraternities that structure living organisms. They pass on the baton to the social sciences by insisting on what consciousness could bring to light in this field. This encourages humans to be open to the potentialities of others in order to better support life or, more modestly, to suffer less. This consciousness is all the more beautiful as it knows it is 'incomplete'.

4. An ethics of the least evil

No one can surf the waves of reality with impunity while ignoring the laws that govern its dynamics. When a civilisation is built on principles or values that are in flagrant contradiction with the reality of this world there is a real danger. That is why our civilisations are deadly. Our most generous and fanciful ideas, and our most subtle and effective techniques emerge from Nature but they are often only epiphenomena. After all, boulders only impede the torrent's flow for a short while!

Thus, the Shiism of the Islamic Republic of Iran will not resist the power of the Persian civilisation for long. As for Saudi Arabia's Wahhabism and its Salafist variants, we can only hope that the civilisation of the desert nomads will soon forget these bloodthirsty follies. Have we not forgotten the follies of the Roman Catholic Inquisition, as well as others perpetrated in the name of religious and political fundamentalism? The twenty-first century will not be religious; it will either be attentive to the mysteries of Being or it won't!

Humanity should strive to gain more scholarly representations of the global dynamics of the world. Yet for a whole host of reasons, this will not be easy. In the meantime, an ethics of the least evil might best guide our thoughts and re-set our moral compasses. The purpose of this section is to define its mind.

Of course, this does not mean admiring everything that Nature can produce. As we have repeatedly pointed out, this could only be a very imperfect achievement of the potentialities of Being, which can not always be relied upon. Acting with conscience, humans would therefore have the responsibility to alleviate the suffering of living things and to consider, more generally, the ethics that must govern any manipulation of the living.

Should we let a child who is severely disabled come into the world? Should genetic mutations be left to the random cosmic particles bombarding the genome? Certainly not! But then again, can we trust humans to the point of allowing them to modify certain 'hot spots' in the genome or even irreversibly modify their germline? The answer is not so simple. Recent studies in the field of embryogensis conducted in the USA, China and Japan show that the field of 'human repair to human augmentation' is a controversial topic.

And then there we have epigenetics, we already know that some traumas, particularly psychological ones, can disrupt the genome. Benefits such as socio-economic ones and education in particular, shape our future at this very deep level. Fraternity is therefore involved in conscience and a deep and warm humanism which is always in the process of becoming and which is our responsibility! We can no longer let life pass us by simply looking with religious or philosophical compassion at its unacceptable achievements, such as that of a human with two heads.

In order to think about fraternity, or a fraternity whose conceptual contours will always be vague, we must first anchor it on what we have instinctively, or through intensive study, come to understand about Nature and not on preconceived ideas that come to us via some random laws revealed to whomever is entitled.

For example, we believe that peaceful euthanasia should be a basic human right even if the individual is in good health; the dignity of his/her condition is at stake. For example, article 3 of the Universal Declaration of Human Rights could be amended, as follows:

> Everyone has the right to life, liberty and security of person and a peaceful and assisted death if that person explicitly requests it.

Apologising for our presence in the world is perhaps the first step on the path towards greater wisdom. The views of the main institutionalised religions, especially in their ecumenical reactionary positions, should not be taken into account; their representations of the world are woefully out of date.

In its deepest sense, this fraternity is part of a certain 'morphology of the unavoidable'. Naturally, genetics and epigenetics, like many other factors, are involved in this morphology but there can be no reductionism in this respect. Fraternity is open while nevertheless being constrained by the potentialities of quantum electrodynamics within our biosphere. Even if these potentialities are objectively considerable, the choices and possible evolutions are indecipherable; they are channelled without it being clear how.

So let us start by listening to what Nature tells us about conception and the arrival into the world of a new human: it is a single bud on the branch of hominids of a strange germination that started (according to the latest news) about three million years ago. It is an adventure in the making. It is unfinished even if it is already incredibly elaborate. By the same token it also means that the potential of a human embryo and an unborn child is unique.

In principle, we should therefore strive to ensure that the 'spectra [3] of potential' of everyone is as varied and extensive as possible; unique, of course, and not too unequal *a priori*. Naturally, we are not unaware of the issues that could arise from the possibilities of related genetic manipulation. Let us not be accused of eugenics! We simply want to convey that

---

3. Here, the meaning of 'spectrum' is that used in physics e.g. the spectrum of sunlight.

participating in the conception of another human is an act of overwhelming responsibility.

Whatever efforts we might make to correct some of Nature's grosser errors whether innate or acquired, the fact remains that any achievement of the living is risky in terms of the process of becoming and is thus incomplete. For example, when MOZART composed his clarinet concerto, a marvellous achievement of the potentialities of his quantum electrodynamics, surely there is something sublime about it and something absolutely complete and accomplished. Of course, but only in terms of the possibilities of the human brain in music. For some other activities, his brain was not as brillant. This is true for many other geniuses who fascinate us, such as the poet Arthur RIMBAUD, the physicist Ettore MAJORANA [4] or the mathematician Alexandre GROTHENDIECK.

To make Living Together truly work, we must ensure that all these talents resonate with our potentialities as far as possible. That is, quite simply, the fraternity of the incomplete! More specifically, we must ensure that the human potential arising from our diverse encounters, whether real or virtual, can flourish.

The fraternity we are talking about here goes beyond our formal thought or emotional systems at the time of these encounters. Education must fight against obscurantism in

---

4. This remarkable physicist and somewhat unusual man disappeared suddenly in the spring of 1938 aged 32; did he commit suicide or run away to South America? Either way, he has never been heard of again. FERMI said of him: "There are several categories of scientists in the world; those of second or third rank who do their best but never get very far. Then there is the first rank, those who make important discoveries, fundamental to scientific progress. But then there are the geniuses like GALILEO and NEWTON. Majorana was one of these.

a spirit of fraternity. However, fraternity can not be forced upon us, we can only establish the conditions for its emergence as in Denmark where pupils are taught about empathy from primary school onwards. This is how we can intuitively develop our capacity to place ourselves in another's shoes to feel what they feel. But if our potential is not compatible with that of another, it goes without saying that real fraternal encounters are not possible. For example, we can have fraternal feelings for those who have had an obscurantist education and not be remotely fraternal with the practitioners of hermeneutics of the powers which impose it and which must be fought mercilessly.

The concept of a fraternity of the incomplete is in fact dictated to us by the observation of what Nature does best. It encourages us to promote a warm and generous freedom based on an ever-changing altruistic equality. Under tragic conditions, this fraternity has led to certain remarkable individuals committing suicide and while this is sad their lives live on deep within our souls just as we remember those who died fighting Nazi barbarism for example. Fraternity is sometimes also "La vie que s'interdit la vie" [NB: the life that life forbids] the title of a collection poems by René NELLI [5].

More modestly, 'being fraternal' means apologising for being what we are, even if we are potentially far more; it means having a deep respect for each other's potential even going as far as seeking it out from deep within their being.

Therefore, wherever our talents or virtues lie and whether we are alive or dead, we are all incomplete. Our fraternal greetings, real or virtual, are shared signs of the

---

5. R. NELLI, « La vie que s'interdit la vie », Ed. Encres Vives (Colomiers).

incompleteness of our existential paths. Nevertheless, these signs of companionship mean that several paths are always better than one, even if we clearly perceive the profound vanity of each of them. We do so in the contained and reserved hope of a better future. This is what we can positively call the 'fraternity of the incomplete'.

Can we live and try to be 'together' in a world whose essence we will never understand; the possible sense of the 'thing-in-itself'? The response must be yes. Ever more sophisticated representations of the world should gradually lead us towards a more serene form of humanity; an ephemeral humanity, but one that is sheltered for a time from the innate storm of violence of the laws of Nature.

Towards the end of ELECTRA, an incredibly tragic play by Jean GIRAUDOUX [6], we find the following beautiful dialogue, which this essay simply echoes.

> *Woman Narses*: Where are we, my poor Electra, where are we?
> *Electra*: Where are we?
> *Woman Narses*: Yes, explain! I never catch on fast. Obviously I sense that something is happening but I don't know what. What is it called when the day rises, like today, when everything is ruined, and everything is pillaged, and nonetheless the air breathes, and one has lost everything, the city burns, the innocents kill each other, but the guilty are in agony in a corner of the day that is rising?
> *Electra*: Ask the beggar. He knows.
> *The beggar*: That has a very pretty name, woman Narses. It's called dawn.

---

6. J. GIRAUDOUX, Électre, Ed. Grasset, 1967.